Creating Prosperity and Abundance

Also by Eliza-Jane Jackson:

Why Doesn't the Law of Attraction Work?

Create Your Own Prosperity Wheel (A step-by-step guide to using the Law of Attraction to manifest the things you want)

Publisher: Shepherd Creative Learning

Creating Prosperity and Abundance
By: Eliza-Jane Jackson

Copyright

Publisher's Note

Please note that much of this publication is based on the author's personal experiences and anecdotal evidence. The views expressed in this book are those of the author, or those who have contributed their story.

The author has made every reasonable attempt to achieve complete accuracy of the content in this Guide, prior to going to press. The publisher, the author and the editor cannot accept responsibility for any errors or omissions, however caused.

You should use this information as you see fit, and at your own risk. Use your own wisdom as guidance. Nothing in the Guide is intended to replace common sense, legal, medical or other professional advice. This Guide is meant to inform and entertain the reader.

No responsibility for loss or damage occasioned to any person acting, or refraining from action, as a result of the material in this publication can be accepted by the publisher, the author or the editor.

Dedication

This book is dedicated to Rosemary Jackson and Dennis Shepherd.

To mum, thank you for your unstinting support and belief in me; especially in my early life when I didn't believe in myself.

To Dennis, thank you for your support and practical help in getting this project off the ground. It's been a pleasure to work with you on this project.

Love to you both, always

To everyone else who has contributed to this book in some way - many thanks. I hope you're manifesting all the things you want. I'm sure you will be an inspiration for others.

About the Author

Eliza-Jane is a successful business consultant, freelance business trainer, holistic life coach, facilitator and author. In short; a very grounded individual.

She doesn't look like a new age traveller or an ageing hippy. However, she has been a spiritual explorer for most of her life. This has included various forms of meditation, prosperity work and the power of positive thinking.

Growing up in a household where one parent had no religious or spiritual beliefs and the other parent had deep spiritual beliefs provided an interesting and thought provoking environment for a curious mind.

From an early age Eliza-Jane has been interested in trying to influence the direction of her life. At first she wasn't aware that it had a name - the Law of Attraction.

Like millions of other people, Eliza-Jane saw The Secret documentary and read the book. Long before that she was captivated by the idea of 'attracting success' through the power of the mind.

As a child she used to write requests on scraps of paper. Intuition told her she needed to express her wishes in this way. Now we call these requests cosmic orders.

Extensive research on the 'Law of Attraction' and 'Cosmic Ordering' prompted her to take a more structured approach. At this point she started creating her own Prosperity Wheels (Visions Boards) and she's never looked back since.

"I don't claim to be a 'guru' but, based on my own experiences, I feel that I have something valuable to share with you... that will help you to enjoy more of the life you want.

I hope you have as much fun with your prosperity work as I have. Thank you for reading my book" (Eliza-Jane Jackson).

Table of Contents

Preface

There are hundreds (possibly even thousands) of books and articles on the subject of prosperity and abundance. So why have I chosen to write 'Creating Prosperity and Abundance'? Lots of the information available focuses on a single element of the Law of Attraction. This is great if you're looking for something specific.

However, if you're new to prosperity work the choice can be overwhelming and may stop you exploring any further.

Manifesting prosperity and abundance is the result of harnessing the Law of Attraction. The Law of Attraction is a very broad topic. It has a common theme though - prosperity and abundance can seriously improve the quality of everyone's life.

Obviously I have no right to try interfering with anyone else's life path or energy. However, I would like to raise awareness of this fascinating subject so more people can make informed choices. If just one person has a more abundant life as a result of this book I will have achieved something.

From a very young age I've been interested in the Law of Attraction, although I didn't know its name. For as long as I can remember I wanted to know who decided what level of poverty or abundance we should have. I also wanted to know why some people seemed to be content with their lives and others were always searching for something.

Obviously my first port of call was my parents. In my teens I started questioning my maternal grandfather as he was a great spiritual believer. I questioned each of them endlessly.

Each question led to yet more questions, which set me on my lifelong interest in spiritual exploration. I'm still learning and enjoying my journey enormously.

With my learning has come a deeper spiritual belief. My life feels more abundant than it did previously, but more importantly I have found inner peace and contentment. I live by the rules of prosperity and abundance, which means others benefit too.

'Creating Prosperity and Abundance' won't answer all your questions. It's not designed to provide in-depth information on any specific part of prosperity work either. I wrote 'Creating Prosperity and Abundance' as a starting point for people new to prosperity work.

Part one of the book deals with the foundations. This includes the principles of prosperity, dealing with clutter and clearing, and creating the right environment for prosperity and abundance.

Part two is the creative part. I've included a chapter on money, cosmic ordering, affirmations, colour, herbs and foods, and power animals. Each is a tool for manifesting prosperity and abundance. You can try one prosperity tool, or use several of them.

The final part of the book deals with gratitude. This is the most important part of prosperity work. Gratitude creates a strong vibration, which creates a continuous prosperity cycle.

There is an ever growing move towards enlightenment and consciousness. Suddenly our very physical and materialist world is losing some of its appeal for many people. You don't need to give up material goods to find enlightenment. Far from it; with enlightenment comes prosperity and abundance in every aspect of your life.

With enlightenment comes spiritual growth. This is turn opens our minds to the possibility that financial wealth and material goods aren't the only goals worth achieving. We can all choose to live an abundant life. Now seems like an ideal time to write a book introducing prosperity and abundance to new readers.

I hope 'Creating Prosperity and Abundance' will leave you curious to find out more.

I welcome feedback, positive or negative. If you have any questions I'm more than happy to try to answer them. If you would like to get in touch, my email address is shepherdcreativelearning@gmail.com.

Part One

"The strongest single factor in prosperity consciousness is self-esteem. Believing you can do it, believing you deserve it, believing you will get it." Jerry Gilles (author of Money Love)

1. Introduction

Creating a beautiful life is your highest calling. Beauty is all around you. It's in the ordinary and overlooked details of the everyday that beauty is revealed, sustained and nurtured.

Sometimes we stumble through life and miss the beauty around us. How often do you acknowledge what a beautiful country we live in? Do you ever feel grateful to live in a country with some of the most incredible scenery in the world?

For many people the word prosperity means financial wealth. Real and lasting prosperity goes much deeper than your bank account. True prosperity is a state of mind, not just financial success or an abundance of material goods.

Abundance also means something different to each of us. Abundance applies to love, power, knowledge, material goods, spirituality, health, a sense of wellbeing, or anything else that's important to you. All of these are aspects of personal abundance.

Prosperity and abundance is available to anyone who has the consciousness and ability to attract all that their heart desires. No two people will share exactly the same ideas of what represents prosperity and abundance. Don't fall into the trap of thinking your idea of prosperity and abundance is the same as everyone else's.

Not everyone will have what appears to be a truly abundant life. Know that this is their choice (conscious or not). There are many reasons why people don't achieve conventional prosperity and abundance. Scarcity is often created for the following reasons:

Self-limiting beliefs

Inability to receive

Inability to clearly visualise what you want

You don't believe you are worthy of the best the Universe can offer

You don't truly believe that you will manifest what you have asked for

Prosperous people generally experience good physical health, emotional wellbeing, inner peace, and feel connected to a greater reality. True abundance reaches every corner of your life. I hope this will inspire you to take a closer look at prosperity and abundance.

Is your glass half full or half empty? It's your view of life that determines your attitude, and the outcome. Buddha summed it up when he said "we are what we think. All that we are arises with our thoughts. With our thoughts we make our world".

We all want to be happy but what is happiness? Have you been brought up to believe you can't have it all? Perhaps you have been brought up believing that in order to get something you have to work hard for it.

I think it's time to dispel some of these old ways of thinking. Everyone's idea of happiness is different. You can't have it all if your expectations are wholly unrealistic.

With a little compromise we can all have the things that matter most to us. You don't have to work hard to get everything you want. Equally, hard work alone won't give you everything you desire.

Everyone can have a life of abundance if they choose to. The Universe has plenty for everyone. There is no witchcraft or anything dubious involved in the process. Manifesting prosperity and abundance can be achieved easily by following these simple steps:

1. Identify what's truly important to you

2. Visualise your goals very clearly. See them as if they are already a reality

3. Show the Universe that you're willing to do your bit to achieve your goals. You can't win the Lottery if you don't buy a Lottery ticket

4. Believe absolutely, not just 99%, that you will achieve your goals

5. Stay focused on what you want

6. Spot opportunities when they knock on your door. We've all missed opportunities as we've failed to recognise them

7. When you manifest what you want, remember to be grateful. Gratitude is probably the most important element of any prosperity work

You are in control of your prosperity or scarcity at all times (even if you're not aware of it). Whether you are living a life of abundance or scarcity is down to you.

Everything that you have or don't have right now is the result of a message you put out to the Universe. This could even be a request sent before you were born. If you're going through a particularly difficult time this can be a hard concept to accept. Your higher consciousness is much more powerful than your conscious mind.

All abundance comes from the same source, and it has nothing to do with religion. Everything is energy and comes from this great source. This includes life, light, money, love, material goods, sense of wellbeing etc. The Universe is the Creator and provider of all energy.

Each of us will find different methods of manifesting our idea of abundance. Personally, I use prosperity wheels (vision boards) and cosmic orders as my core prosperity tools. I also like to use colour, meditation, crystals, and power animals.

Your prosperity and abundance is only limited by your imagination. If you stop visualising and believing you will stop manifesting what you desire. So, be creative and visualise, visualise, visualise! The supply is limitless.

One of the most valuable components of successful manifestation is 'blind faith'. It's essential to believe that you're going to achieve something that isn't currently physically present. For people new to prosperity work this can be the toughest part.

Some may argue that controlling what you do or don't have in life is messing with your life purpose. I disagree. The more enlightened I become the more I feel that I'm on my life path.

I've also noticed that as I become more attuned to what the Universe has to offer I develop spiritually. My current view of abundance is less materialist than it was when I first began my prosperity work. Other spiritual explorers that I've met report similar experiences.

Please read this book with an open mind. You don't have to believe everything that is written here – just explore as a scientist would do. If you read the book and don't like the things you manifest, stop. You can revert to manifesting through subconscious thought any time you like. It really is as simple as that.

Please note: the Universe, the Source, the Creator and God are all the same thing. This is the source from which all energy comes. As everything is energy, this is the source from which all prosperity and abundance comes.

"Prosperity makes friends, adversity tries them" Publilius Syrus

2. The Principles of Prosperity and Abundance

When someone says the words 'prosperity' or 'abundance' do you automatically think about money? If so, let's dispel this myth straightaway.

Prosperity or abundance isn't all about money. It means different things to each of us. Prosperity and abundance is a state of mind. The more you apply the principles of prosperity and abundance the less important money becomes. You will find out more about this is chapter 6.

One key thing you need to know about the principle of abundance is – there is plenty for everyone. None of us needs to struggle or harm others in order to succeed. I know this is hard to comprehend when you hear about so much poverty in the world.

Prosperity and abundance is available to everyone, but we can only ask for ourselves. You shouldn't ask for prosperity and abundance for other people as this interferes with their energy.

In terms of Universal Laws this interference is wholly unacceptable; even if you did it with good intentions. None of us has the right to interfere with someone else's energy.

Everyone has a different view on the principles of prosperity and abundance. I've chosen to include the Zen Masters' five principles of abundance as these sum it up well. These are:

1. The Universe (the Creator or God) doesn't discriminate while giving. We are all equal and have the same chances to access prosperity and abundance. Whether you're a good or bad person you can have what you want. You just need to know how to ask for it

2. What you can achieve is only limited by your aspirations and imagination. There is no limit to what the Universe can provide if you know how to ask for it. Once you have mastered this principle the world is your oyster

3. Your words and thoughts multiply 100 times. If you speak and think positive thoughts they will multiply. Equally, if you speak and think negative thoughts they will multiply

4. Each intention (belief) creates a vibration. If your intention is strong enough you will manifest what you visualise. This works equally well with positive and negative thoughts, so choose what you want to visualise with care. The stronger the vibration the quicker you will manifest your heart's desires

5. Clutter blocks energy. Clutter can be physical, emotional or spiritual. Clutter is anything you carry in your life that has no value right now. See chapter 4 for more information about clutter

Exercise: The Things That Exist in Abundance on Earth

Abundance is all around us, but all too often we fail to see it. We aren't deliberately blind to abundance. We just seem to walk through life looking for something and failing to appreciate what's already here.

Try this exercise to see how aware you are of the abundance around you:

1. Create a list of all the things that are in abundance on the earth

2. Which of these do you appreciate?

3. What makes you happy? This is a personal experience so you won't find the answer on the internet

4. What have you learnt from this exercise?

Your answers to question 1 might include trees, grass, sand, water, flowers, insects, animals, birds, fish and people. Equally, you may have come up with an extensive list of things I haven't included.

Each of these exists because they give back to the Creator in some way. This keeps them perpetuating. Take grass for example. Grass provides food for other life forms. It also creates seeds that enable more grass to grow.

Imagine a world without judgement – that is exactly what the Universe is. The Universe doesn't judge whether you're worthy of prosperity and abundance or not. The Universe sends prosperity and abundance where it's invited and welcomed.

Unfortunately, our society is only pleased to see people succeed when they achieve their success through hardship and struggle. Obviously you can't change the mindset of those around you, but you can change your own mindset.

You can learn to be pleased for others and show gratitude for what you have. The more gratitude you demonstrate, the more prosperity and abundance you will attract.

True abundance will not deprive someone else to give you what you want. Anyone can generate prosperity and abundance. To achieve what you want you have to be able to visualise, believe and manifest.

You do need to be able to notice when you manifest what you want. This sounds obvious, but too often people get into the mindset of wanting. They fail to notice when they are manifesting and so keep wanting.

For some people prosperity and abundance is about money or financial wealth. For others it may be career success, love, material goods, health, knowledge, or a life devoted to serving others. No two people have the same prosperity and abundance blueprint. Focus on what you want, not wanting for others.

The Universe has never asked us to struggle or turn ourselves into martyrs. Mother Teresa chose to live a life without great financial wealth. However, she did not live a life of poverty; far from it. Although she paid for economy flights whenever she travelled, airlines upgraded her to first class because of who she was.

Wherever Mother Teresa went people wanted to do things for her and help her. This was because of the good she was doing in the world. This created a win/win outcome. Therefore, Mother Teresa led a prosperous life even though she didn't contrive to make this happen.

True prosperity is always win-win outcome. Mother Teresa is one of the best examples of true prosperity and abundance.

Whatever you choose your ability to experience abundance, happiness, peace or harmony is an internal job. You need to consciously and consistently tell the Universe what you want.

Everything you have or don't have is as a result of a consistent message sent to the Universe previously. Metaphysicians have long known that we create our experiences with our beliefs. If you believe that you're destined to struggle, you will experience this.

Exercise: My Negative Thoughts

Consider the following statement for a moment. "Everything you have or don't have is the result of a consistent message you sent to the Universe".

1. Think of a time in your life when you were focused on scarcity, lack or poverty. For example, perhaps you struggled to get a job. Were you constantly broke.

2. Visualise this experience as clearly as possible and replay it in your mind. Remember how it felt like an ever decreasing spiral

3. What eventually changed the situation?

Most people break out of their negative cycle because the pain becomes unbearable. They finally feel they have to do something about it. That's when they start to look for a positive solution. As the vibration changes from negative to positive so does the outcome.

Every thought creates a vibration. Some are fleeting and so don't create anything. Others are strong and so create an outcome. The Universe simply responds to the vibration your thoughts create.

Clear, focused energy that flows freely is more likely to create positive and enjoyable results. Negative thoughts characterised by struggles and blockages will simply create scarcity as that is what you're focusing on.

Unfortunately, all too often people say "I don't want..." The effect is the same as saying positive affirmations. You will end up manifesting the things you don't actually want in your life. I'm sure you've heard the expression "be careful what you wish for". From now on just focus on the things you do want.

True abundance comes from asking with positive intent. A cautionary note – you should not ask for anything that will harm or deprive someone else.

Of course, not everyone plays by this set of rules, but this is their decision. They will have to deal with the consequences. Don't get caught up in passing judgement on others as this may have a negative impact on your own prosperity.

Changing to a positive mindset may be difficult to accept. Once you do adopt a positive attitude you can have whatever you want. Just ask for it in a way that can be understood by the Universe. Generally, a single thought will not be sufficient to manifest.

Mark Victor Hansen and Robert Allen have included an interesting comment in 'The One Minute Millionaire'. Quote: "there is an ocean of abundance and one can tap into it with a teaspoon, a bucket or a tractor and trailer. The ocean doesn't care". Think about this for a moment.

The final principle of abundance is dealing with the physical, emotional and spiritual clutter in our lives. I have devoted a chapter to this topic as it needs properly addressing if you want to achieve prosperity and abundance. Chapter 4 deals with clutter and clearing.

"Everyone creates realities based on their own personal beliefs. These beliefs are so powerful that they can create [expansive or entrapping] realities over and over." Kuan Yin

3. Inflowing and Outflowing Energy

The entire physical Universe is made up of energy in different forms. The prosperity cycle also consists of energy. It's made up of a combination of inflowing and outflowing energy.

The energy that flows through you helps to define the quality of your life. It also defines your physical, emotional, spiritual, and financial experiences.

In order to be truly prosperous and abundant you need a healthy balance of both inflowing and outflowing energy. Too much emphasis on either inflowing or outflowing energy will result in an energy blockage. This prevents prosperity and abundance manifesting in your physical world.

When you eat and digest your food the excess needs to be removed to keep you healthy. Energy works in the same way. The prosperity energy you take in needs to be slightly greater than what you release. However, the two sides must be almost equal to maintain a balanced prosperity cycle.

Everyone's idea of prosperity and abundance is different. What feels like abundance to you may not be to others. Don't try to force your views on others; just respect their opinions. True prosperity and abundance comes easily once you have a genuine sense of wellbeing.

Later in this chapter I have suggested ways to keep your prosperity energy flowing and balanced. First let's deal with inflowing and outflowing energy.

Inflowing Energy

The prosperity cycle begins with inflowing energy. After all, you can't give if you've got nothing.

Inflow energy may manifest itself in lots of different ways. Your inflow energy may come as money, financial gains or material goods. Equally, it may manifest as compliments, love, nurturing, feelings and emotions or a sense of wellbeing. For some inflow energy is presented as increased spiritual awareness.

The point I'm making is we're all different. Therefore, our perception of inflow energy and the benefits will be different. Learn to understand yourself better and recognise your inflow energy.

There is no limit to the inflow energy you can receive. However, you do need to be open to receiving and appreciate what you have. Furthermore, you need to be able to recognise abundance when it happens.

Begin by learning to be a little kinder to yourself. Do you treat yourself how you want others to treat you? Are you kinder, more tolerant and more sympathetic to other people than you are to yourself? Most people are.

Next, start to focus on creating more of the things you want. This may be more time, money, material goods, love or anything else that you feel is lacking in your life right now. Imagine you already have what you want. Feel how great it is to have your heart's desires.

A word of warning; it's not enough to be open to receiving abundance. You also need to be open to allowing others to receive abundance too. Jealousy can be a hard habit to break.

It can be very hard to genuinely wish the best for everyone you meet. It's especially hard if others seem to have more than you. If you want to achieve true prosperity and abundance for yourself you have to wish the best for everyone. This is one of the rules of the Law of Attraction.

"No people ever yet benefitted by riches if their prosperity corrupted their virtue." Theodore Roosevelt

Does your subconscious constantly tell you that others are unworthy of their prosperity? If so the chances are, at a very deep subconscious level, you feel that you're unworthy too. This attitude creates an automatic blockage to abundance, which will significantly slow your progress.

Back to your inflowing energy, there are three possible levels of receiving prosperity and abundance:

Level 1 - You receive exactly what you want and everything is now perfect

Level 2 - You receive what you thought you wanted, but now you're not sure if this is what you wanted after all

Level 3 - You don't receive what you want or you receive something entirely different

The first outcome (level 1) is great. You must remember to continue visualising in order to maintain the same level of prosperity and abundance.

Level two is probably OK, or at least it has proved to you that the process works. Levels one and two mean you can move forward by defining new goals. There is no limit to what you can ask for.

The third outcome is a different matter. This says your conscious and unconscious states are not aligned with each other. Perhaps you aren't ready for what you have asked for. Or, during the process your needs and wants changed. Finally, you didn't state your desired outcome clearly enough for the Universe to deliver what you wanted.

Look again at what you truly want, and shift your focus slightly. Just doing this can make a difference. Alternatively, choose something else to work on and see what happens. With clear intentions and a strong belief everyone can achieve prosperity and abundance.

The Universe always delivers what it thinks we asked for. This is why our conscious and unconscious states must be aligned. Otherwise the Universe will respond to your vibration not your conscious declarations.

The other thing about inflow energy is - we have to give the Universe a helping hand. Don't simply have a thought and then sit back and expect the Universe to deliver. You need to play your part too.

Whenever you ask for something decide what you're willing to do to make it happen. For example, do you want to win the Lottery? If so, you need to buy a Lottery ticket. How else can the Universe deliver what you want?

How grateful are you for the things you receive? Here's an exercise to help you assess how much you appreciate what you have. This exercise needs to be done over the period of a week.

Exercise: Give Yourself a Treat

Give yourself a treat every day for a week. This could be something small like a single chocolate or 10 minutes 'me time'. If you want to give yourself something more indulgent why not try flowers, books, magazines, clothes or jewellery etc. It really doesn't matter what the gift is; it's the process of giving that matters.

At the end of your week long exercise reflect on how you feel. If the exercise has worked you should be feeling a little more nurtured. If not, you may need to repeat this exercise.

Are you one of those people who struggles to receive? Some people find it much easier to give than to receive. This creates an imbalance in your inflow and outflow energy. It also creates an imbalance for the person who is trying to give you something. If this is your issue you need to learn to be a gracious receiver.

The Universe is very literal. It responds to the vibration your words create. The Universe isn't capable of reading the hidden message.

If you don't accept gifts the Universe will assume that you don't want to receive prosperity and abundance. The Universe will oblige by giving your more scarcity.

Visualise yourself receiving all kinds of gifts and compliments. Don't reject them. Instead practice smiling and saying "Thank you", or "Thanks, I'll put it to good use" or "Thanks, I really appreciate this". Be open to receiving as this creates a win/win outcome.

Exercise: Learn To Be a Gracious Receiver

If being a gracious receiver doesn't feel natural to you then you may need to work on this. If you can't be grateful and gracious about what you receive you will limit your prosperity and abundance.

1. Next time someone gives you a compliment accept it graciously. Don't reject it or dismiss it. Just enjoy the compliment for a few minutes, safe in the knowledge that it was a sincere gesture

2. When family, friends or colleagues try to do something for you don't block them. Accept these kind offers and enjoy the gift in the spirit it's given

3. Ask for help when you need it. No one is superman or superwoman

4. Accept gifts and presents without saying "oh you shouldn't have..."

5. Develop an attitude of gratitude for every gift or compliment you receive

6. You should get as much pleasure from receiving as you get from giving

7. Keep a log of all the nice things people do for you or compliments you receive. Also make a note of your response. Did you accept it graciously or reject it? Do this for a month and see how you feel at the end of it.

If you still struggle with receiving graciously you may need to extend this exercise over a longer period. This is probably a habit that has been developed over a lifetime. In order to progress the habit must be stopped.

Outflowing Energy

This is just as important as inflowing energy. Just as the energy enters the prosperity cycle through the inflow so it needs to leave through the outflow. If this doesn't happen freely and in a balanced way the energy becomes trapped. Eventually your prosperity and abundance will cease or significantly slow down.

Some people give too much while others give too little. Both create a prosperity imbalance that will negatively impact your sense of physical, emotional or spiritual abundance.

Don't over give as this depletes your supply. No one benefits if you over give and then end up feeling resentful when you don't get as much back.

The Universe is then lulled into believing that you would rather give than receive. It will then provide you with more opportunities to give and get little in return. As you can see this would not produce a good long-term outcome for you.

Spending money is the most obvious way to outflow your prosperity and abundance, but it's not the only way. After all, money isn't the only thing you can give. Sometimes giving your professional services, moral support, material goods, or giving your time freely is more valuable.

On other occasions money is what is really needed. Be honest about what is needed and give accordingly; rather than what you want to give. Genuine giving (outflowing prosperity energy) is about the recipient not you.

If you give time and friendship when money is needed you will be repaid in kind. The Universe will give you time and friendship as it sees this is important to you. If you want to receive money you have to be willing to give money.

Whenever you give (of yourself, money or goods) do so sincerely and without expecting anything in return. Unconditional sharing keeps your emotional inflow and outflow energy in balance. Have faith that you will always have enough. This will remove the fear of scarcity.

Never give to the point you have nothing left. This will have a negative impact on your physical, emotional or spiritual prosperity level. Never give conditionally either.

Giving too much should never be confused with unconditional giving. Over giving is a trained response where you have been taught to take care of others before yourself. This can also be a way of asking for love or trying to control others. Either way, this isn't a healthy habit to adopt.

Exercise: Are You an Excessive Giver?

As I've already said, it's important to strike the right balance between giving and receiving. Answer the following questions to see if you're guilty of giving too much:

1. Are you mostly surrounded by takers?

2. Do you find it difficult to accept compliments or gifts? Do you tend to bat compliments away? Do you say "oh you shouldn't have" when someone gives you a gift?

3. Do you ever refuse to accept money that is owed to you?

4. Do you feel you have to be the responsible one where money is concerned?

5. How do you feel about spending time or money on yourself?

6. Why do you feel the need to do more for others than they do for you? Although this question requires some soul searching and deep honesty; it's the only way forward

7. Do you feel guilty about having or wanting money?

Review your answers to these questions. The chances are you were already aware of your attitude to giving. Hopefully this has made you face the reality.

It's up to you whether you choose to balance your giving and receiving. If you continue to give more than you receive you will never achieve a prosperity and abundance balance.

Instead of over giving you may not like giving at all. Deep down inside, excessive takers don't believe they are good enough. Subconsciously excessive takers believe getting people to do things for them will eventually lead them to feel worthy of prosperity and abundance. Unfortunately, it doesn't work like this.

Are you wondering if you're an excessive taker? If so try this quick exercise.

Exercise: Am I An Excessive Taker?

It's very important that you answer these questions truthfully. You may feel uncomfortable if you find out you're an excessive taker. If so, see it as an opportunity to change:

1. Do you rarely give compliments to others?

2. Do you rarely buy gifts for others?

3. Are you too busy taking care of yourself to care about how your actions affect other people?

4. Do you often refuse to leave a tip?

5. Do you expect others to do more for you than you're willing to do for them?

6. Do you grudge what you do for others?

7. Do you spend most of your time and money focusing on yourself and neglecting your obligation to others?

8. Are you quick to complain about others but respond badly to criticism about yourself?

9. Do you often delegate your obligations to others?

This exercise is not a stick to beat you with. It's an opportunity to take an objective look at yourself.

If you have always been a taker, try sharing for a change. This might feel slightly uncomfortable to start with, but stick with it and very soon it will feel natural. Here's an exercise in giving to help get you started.

Exercise: Learning To Give

If you aren't naturally a giver then it's a habit you need to learn. This exercise will help to get you started. Simply work through these instructions over a period of days or weeks.

1. Spend a few minutes each day visualising what it's like to be a giver instead of a taker. Visualise doing something good for people who have done things for you in the past

2. When you feel comfortable with the visualisation, try practising it for real. Notice the impact your generosity has on others

3. Learn to be kinder to yourself as well as others. Start with compliments to yourself. This costs nothing and doesn't require forethought. Notice how nice positive thoughts feel

4. Next, make a list of all your qualities and put the list somewhere you will see it regularly. The fridge door is an ideal place

Note: I know this may not feel comfortable initially, but stick with it

5. You may find yourself adding to the list over the next few days or weeks. Look at your list several times each day. Each time you look at your list pay yourself a sincere compliment

6. Practice this exercise for at least 30 days, so it becomes a habit you're comfortable with

You may be wondering what you can give. Here are some suggestions to get you started:

Give a compliment to at least one person each day. Make sure the compliment is sincere

Give a small amount of money to charity each month by setting up a Direct Debit or Standing Order. Don't grudge doing this as it will negate your action

Each time you receive small change put it into the nearest charity collection box. This may be just a couple of pennies but the gesture matters to the Universe

Make a list of all the people who mean most to you. Do something nice for at least one of them each month

Make more effort to keep in touch with family and friends

Join a 'Reading in Schools' programme and help a child improve his/her reading skills

Do some voluntary work for a couple of hours each month

Give your professional services or time freely to someone who needs it. Mentoring is a great way to help a new business or help someone with their career

Now you're getting the hang of giving you might like to create a giving plan.

Exercise: Create a Giving Plan

A giving plan is an excellent way to ensure giving becomes a natural action. Unconditional giving is a good way to maintain a healthy balance of inflowing and outflowing energy. The more you give unconditionally the more you will receive.

Here are the instructions for making a giving plan:

1. Make a list of all the 'good causes' that are important to you

2. From this list choose the 'good causes' that mean the most to you. Identify the causes, charities or individuals you would like to give time or money to during the next twelve months

3. You may also like to make a list of possible causes for the future

4. Start to plan what you intend to give each month for the next year. Remember the intention is more important than the amount, so only give what you can afford to give

5. Choose a start date for your giving plan. The sooner you start giving the sooner you will start to receive more yourself

6. Implement your plan and stick to it

7. Review your progress periodically throughout the next twelve months. You should review it quarterly at least

8. At each review consider if you're on track or if your plans need to change

Note: It isn't good karma to declare an intention and then do nothing about it. Be realistic about what time or money you can afford to give, and do it unconditionally.

If you give grudgingly or conditionally it will negatively impact your own future prosperity and abundance. Always bear in mind, the Universe has more than enough for everyone. By giving unconditionally you will be more than rewarded.

Giving and Receiving

It's important to strike the right balance between giving and receiving. Receive first and then give. Although it's 'good to give' it's not good to allow your giving and receiving to get out of balance. An imbalance simply leads to resentment.

In order to get the things you want you have to be willing to receive. Sounds stupid I know, but so many people are obsessed with making it happen. They then forget to allow it to happen.

When you over-give you send a message to the Universe that you prefer to give rather than receive. The Universe responds by giving you more opportunities to give and gain little in return.

Some people struggle with both giving and receiving. They may find it hard to receive compliments or gifts. They may also struggle with sharing their prosperity with others, or simply loving themselves. This often results in a person who is emotionally drained, bitter and generally discontented with their life. These people are not easy to be with.

Exercise: Am I Getting The Balance Right?

Are you getting the balance right between giving and receiving? If you're not sure answer the following questions truthfully:

1. If someone pays you a compliment, what is your reaction? Do you say 'thank you' and smile or do you side-step the remark and put it down?

2. If someone says they like your outfit, do you say "oh this old thing?"

3. If someone says you look good, do you say you feel lousy?

4. If someone says they admire you, do you shrug it off?

5. Do you find it difficult to accept things without giving something in return?

6. Do you rarely spend time or money on yourself?

7. Do you feel you need to do more for others than they do for you?

8. Do you feel guilty about having or wanting money?

If your answers are mainly yes you have a problem with giving and receiving. This means your inflow and outflow energy is out of balance. Without change you will never enjoy all the Universe has to offer.

Meditation has a role to play in energy balancing. Meditation also has many physical health and emotional wellbeing benefits. The Inflow/Outflow Balancing Meditation is a useful exercise to help increase your energy flow. This in turn should increase your prosperity and abundance.

Exercise: Inflow/Outflow Balancing Meditation

Whether you're a seasoned meditator or new to meditation, this exercise is easy to do. Simply follow the instructions below:

1. Breathe in deeply through your nose and then slowly exhale (breathe out) through your mouth

2. With each in/out breath feel your body and mind beginning to relax

3. Repeat this deep breathing until you feel relaxed and peaceful. Now you're ready to start the meditation

4. Visualise yourself sitting on a golden or silver throne. It doesn't matter which you choose

5. Visualise yourself dressed in beautiful clothes (bright colours are good) and adorned with jewels

6. Continue the visualisation by seeing yourself in a room fit for Royalty. Your room is filled with luxury furnishings and beautiful flowers

7. Next see the room filling up with lots of well-wishers. Your well-wishers may be family, friends or even strangers. Everyone is smiling, laughing, telling jokes and generally having a good time

8. Visualise each person approaching you with a gift. This should be everything your heart desires. This could be material goods like cars, houses, flowers etc. It could also be less tangible things like a sense of wellbeing, peace or good health. The choice is yours

9. See yourself thanking each person for the gift they have just given you. Sense the gratitude you feel for the gift and the generosity of the giver

10. As the room empties take time to look at and appreciate all your beautiful gifts

11. Once you have completed this part of the exercise it's time for you to be the bearer of gifts. Remember prosperity is about receiving and giving

12. Visualise yourself, still dressed in your beautiful clothes, visiting a friend or family member. Visualise yourself offering them a gift that you think they would appreciate. This can be anything, large or small. It's important that this gift is something the person would appreciate receiving

13. Next visualise yourself visiting another person and offering them a gift. Once again, it must be something they would like to receive

14. Continue this exercise until you have visited everyone who is important to you. This can be family and friends or even strangers you

want to help. Each gift should be given because you think the receiver will enjoy it

15. Once you have given everyone a gift that you feel they would appreciate notice how good you feel. If the exercise has worked you will feel good about giving and receiving

16. Now visualise yourself returning to your throne and preparing for the next influx of giving and receiving

Note: you can do this exercise as often as you like. Alternatively, do this exercise if you feel like your inflowing and outflowing energy is out of balance.

Balance

You may not be an excessive giver or taker, in which case you're a healthy receiver. You probably already have a healthy balance of inflow and outflow prosperity energy. This is an excellent starting point for manifesting true prosperity and abundance.

Taking care of your needs is just as important as giving money, gifts, time etc to anyone else. If you feel nurtured you will find it much easier to do things for others. You might like to try this happiness budget exercise.

Exercise: Create a Happiness Budget

1. Make a list of all the things that make you happy. Your list should include your physical or health needs, money, time, emotional and spiritual needs. Your list may be extensive and may take several days to complete

2. Set aside a certain amount of money each month for you (see tithing in Chapter 6 - The Money Connection). This can be a nominal sum or something much larger depending upon your personal circumstances

3. Each month choose at least one item from your list and buy yourself this gift. For example you may decide to buy yourself some flowers or chocolates, or have a massage etc

4. Each month also take care of one of your other needs on your happiness budget. This may involve doing something to take care of your

health, emotional or spiritual needs. For example you may choose to go for a walk somewhere special

5. At the end of three, six and twelve months review your happiness budget. Notice how your attitude to taking care of yourself has changed. If the exercise is working for you your attitude to taking care of yourself will have improved

Although you may have a healthy attitude to giving and receiving you might like to do a quick review periodically. This will ensure you maintain a healthy balance of inflowing and outflowing energy. The 'My Personal Balance Sheet' exercise is ideal for doing this.

Exercise: My Personal Balance Sheet

Think back to last week, last month or three months ago. Try to remember your significant giving and receiving during this period. Make a note of anything that stands out in your mind.

1. On a sheet of paper create two columns. The heading for column 1 is 'Received' and the heading for column 2 is 'Given'

2. In the 'Received' column list all your inflowing prosperity. Include compliments from family or friends, personal recommendations, flowers, money or other gifts. This list is anything material or otherwise that you received during this period. If you can't think of anything then you clearly have some issues with receiving that need to be addressed

3. In the 'Given' column list all the gifts you have given to others during this period. This list might include compliments, charitable donations, taking a friend out to lunch, mowing your neighbour's lawn. The list of potential gifts is endless

It's useful to do this exercise periodically as it ensures that your inflow and outflow energy remains in balance. Balance is hugely important if you want to enjoy all the Universe has to offer.

"Prosperity is a way of living and thinking, and not just money or things. Poverty is a way of living and thinking, and not just a lack of money or things." Eric Butterworth

4. Dealing With Clutter and Clearing

When talking about prosperity and abundance clutter is anything that doesn't serve a purpose in your life. Clutter will stifle your ability to move forward. It also makes everything hard work when it doesn't need to be.

Don't be lulled into believing that all clutter is physical. Clutter can be physical, emotional or spiritual. Each can block your prosperity and abundance. You may think clutter is not important in the grand scheme of things, but that's not actually true. Clutter stifles prosperity.

Types of Clutter

Physical clutter may invade your personal or work space, and can take over your life. It's easy to see why this type of clutter blocks prosperity and abundance. It's obvious that energy cannot flow freely in an environment that is full of clutter.

Physical clutter can be far reaching. It may also impact your emotional and spiritual wellbeing. When you throw out the physical clutter you're also starting to clear your mind (an added bonus).

It's often easier to make excuses and find reasons to keep clutter than to make the effort to get rid of it. If you're able to get rid of physical clutter you will open the doors to prosperity and abundance.

Most people report that their physical space feels different after a good declutter. Obviously you will have created some physical space. You will also notice that you feel different.

We all store emotional and spiritual clutter in our bodies, in varying degrees. Emotional clutter is the mental baggage that you acquire over the years. Every life experience creates a memory. Some are positive and some are negative. The negative memories create your emotional clutter.

We all have feelings. These are a physical or mental sensation to something. Feelings are neither good nor bad; they just are feelings. None of us can choose which feelings to have as they are automatic. However, each of us decides whether a feeling is good or bad. Negative feelings become our emotional clutter.

If it helps, think of emotional clutter as dead wood lying in a river. The more branches or logs in the river the less freely the water can flow. If it's totally blocked the water will eventually stagnate.

Emotional clutter can be very draining. It can sap your energy and make it difficult to get things done. Emotional clutter can also prevent the natural flow of prosperity and abundance.

Past emotions that have not been dealt with have a direct effect on your emotional reactions to current situations. If you fail to deal with negative emotions they will stay in your tissues, glands, muscles, organs and systems.

To clear emotional clutter you need to feel the emotion so you can release it. This is why people are often reluctant to do emotional clearing. The process for emotional clearing is:

1. Feel the emotion

2. Accept it. It's an historical event so you can't change it. Accept that sometimes bad things happen

3. Release it to the Universe for cleansing

By releasing your emotional clutter you give yourself permission to be happy. This can be a painful process so only do it when you feel emotionally strong enough.

Spiritual clutter surrounds your soul. Spiritual clutter limits your ability to develop values and actions that are in sync with your life purpose. Spirituality is about truth, dignity, integrity, faith, hope and love. Spiritual clutter in your life stops you living with these values and serving your life purpose.

In order to function fully you need a balance of inflowing and outflowing energy. This balance takes into account your physical and mental state. To be fully receptive to prosperity and abundance your mind, body and soul have to be in harmony with each other.

By removing physical tension and stress your body will be able to relax. This in turn will enable the Universe to bring you the life you want.

The body awareness relaxation exercise may help you to gain a sense of physical and emotional wellbeing.

Exercise: Body Awareness Relaxation Exercise

You don't need to be a regular meditator to do this exercise. Whoever you are, it will help you to enjoy a short period of peace and relaxation.

1. Lie on your back, legs uncrossed, arms straight at your sides and your eyes open or closed

2. Breathe in deeply through your nose. Hold your breath for a count of up to 5 and then exhale very slowly through your mouth

3. Repeat this breathing exercise for a couple of minutes until you feel relaxed

4. When you're relaxed and ready to start. Shift your attention to the toes of your right foot. Take a moment to focus on the way your toes feel

5. Notice any sensations you feel in your toes while continuing to also focus on your breathing. Imagine each deep breath flowing straight to your toes. Repeat this exercise for 1 minute - all the time remaining focused on this area only

6. Move your focus to the sole of your right foot. Tune in to any sensations you feel in that part of your body. Imagine each breath flowing to the sole of your foot. Repeat this exercise for 1 minute - all the time remaining focused on this area

7. Move your focus to your right ankle. Tune in to any sensations you feel in your ankle and imagine each breath flowing to your ankle. Repeat this exercise for 1 minute - all the time remaining focused on this area

8. Repeat this exercise for your right calf, knee, thigh and hip

9. Now switch to your left side. Repeat steps 5-8 on your left side, finishing with your left hip

10. Next, move up your torso. Start with your lower back. Continue to breathe deeply and feel each breathe going straight to your lower back. Take a minute or two to focus on the way it feels

11. Now move onto your abdomen. As you breathe deeply sense your breath reaching your abdomen. Be aware of how it feels. Spend 1 minute focusing on any sensations you feel in your abdomen

12. When you're ready, move to your upper back. Imagine each deep breath flowing to your upper back and releasing the tension. Focus on the way your upper back feels for 1 minute

13. As you continue to breathe deeply, focus your attention on your chest. Imagine each deep breath flowing to your chest. Focus on the way your chest feels for 1 minute

14. Now move onto your shoulders. You might like to spend a little longer on your shoulders as they absorb a lot of tension. As you breathe deeply sense each breath spreading across your shoulders and soothing away any tension. Spend as long as necessary focusing on any sensations you feel in your shoulders and imagine the tension disappearing

15. Next, imagine each deep breath flowing to your fingers on your right hand. Repeat this exercise for 1 minute - all the time remaining focused on your fingers

16. Move your focus to your right hand, moving up to your wrist. Tune in to any sensations you feel in your hand. Imagine each breath flowing to your right hand and wrist. Repeat this exercise for 1 minute - all the time remaining focused on this area

17. Repeat this for your right forearm, elbow and upper arm until it reaches your shoulder. Tune in to any sensations you feel in your arm and imagine each breath flowing through your right arm. Repeat this exercise for 1 minute - all the time remaining focused on your arm

18. Now switch to your left fingers and hand. Repeat steps 15-17 on your left side, finishing at the top of your left arm

19. Next, move through your neck and throat. Imagine your deep breathing soothing these areas and taking all the tension away. Emotional clutter often lodges in the throat area, causing a sore throat or throat infection

20. Finally move onto your face, the back and top of your head. Pay close attention to your jaw, chin, lips, tongue, nose, cheeks, eyes, forehead, temples and scalp. Image each deep breath covering your face and head, and soothing any tension

21. When you reach the very top of your head, let your breath reach out beyond your body. Imagine yourself hovering above your physical body

22. After completing the body awareness relaxation exercise, relax for a few minutes in silence and stillness. While you're doing this notice how relaxed your body feels. When you're ready open your eyes slowly

Cosmic ordering is the process of requesting and manifesting what you want. Usually cosmic ordering fails when something comes between you and your Universal abundance. Generally this is nothing more than an energy blockage or a self-limiting belief, but sometimes it can be due to stress.

The human body is a cosmic record of your memories, experiences and beliefs (clutter). Every loving feeling, joy, hurt, anger or annoyance, is stored until it's released.

It's important to practice physical, emotional and spiritual clearing on a regular basis. This will ensure your inflow and outflow energy maintain a healthy balance. This in turn helps prosperity and abundance to manifest naturally.

If your body is feeling light and free of emotional/spiritual burden you can manifest all the prosperity and abundance you desire. On the other hand, if your body is feeling heavy and tense it's much harder to manifest what you want.

Are you bogged down with emotional or spiritual clutter? If so, it will need to be removed before you can successfully manifest abundance.

Exercise: Are You Bogged Down With Emotional or Spiritual Clutter?

If you're not sure whether you have a problem with emotional or spiritual clutter answer the following questions:

1. Do you understand how your mind and emotions have contributed to the clutter in your life?

2. Do you understand the connection between the physical clutter and emotional and spiritual issues that are present in your life?

3. Do you have difficulty breaking habits that no longer serve a useful purpose in your life?

4. Do you keep revisiting historical issues? Do you have difficulty letting them go?

5. Do you devote much time or effort to self-nurturing? Or, do you find excuses not to take care of yourself?

Physical Clearing

Physical clearing relates to clearing your body as well as your physical environment (home, office, car, garage etc). Physical clearing literally means taking good care of your body and doing something to send the memories away.

Let's start with your physical environment. Clutter in your physical world will make it difficult for the Law of Attraction to work. People often say they want more prosperity and abundance. However, the weight of the energy of the 'old stuff' in their homes prevents this.

Remember all energy needs to be able to flow freely. Maybe it's time to declutter. This will allow the energy and abundance to flow naturally and freely in your physical environment.

Initially you may find it difficult to start decluttering. The sooner you start the sooner you will begin manifesting the prosperity and abundance you desire.

Don't throw everything away just because you need to declutter. This will not get you into the right mindset to manifest abundance. Instead try sorting things into piles or boxes as described below in the physical decluttering exercise.

Exercise: Physical Decluttering Exercise

Start with household items and personal effects. When this task is complete move onto decluttering your clothes, shoes etc.

1. Sort everything into piles or boxes as follows:
Beautiful and/or useful things that you want to keep
Things you don't want but feel they may come in useful one day
Things that should be somewhere else (e.g. charity shop or given away)
Things to be thrown away
Don't knows (this should be few in number)

The things you want to keep should give you joy, serve a useful purpose, or have sentimental value. Don't simply keep things because getting rid of them might cause offence. Remember, this task is about decluttering your physical environment to enable you to manifest the things you truly want.

2. Next look at the things that you think may come in useful one day. Ask yourself "when was the last time I used this?" Be honest, and get rid of all those things that you have not used for at least 12 months

These items, along with the 'should be somewhere else' items can be sent to a charity shop, recycled or sold to raise cash. This will create a win/win outcome.

The rubbish should be disposed of quickly. This will automatically shift the energies in your physical environment.

3. Now you should just be left with a small number of 'don't knows' to deal with. Go through the same exercise you did for the 'may come in useful one day' items. Make a diary note to revisit these items in 6 months' time. By this date you may feel it's the right time to give them away or throw them away.

This exercise can be difficult or stressful if you have not done this before. Be kind to yourself and work at a pace you're comfortable with. Do complete the task, no matter how challenging. This will make manifesting prosperity and abundance so much easier.

4. Next, go through your wardrobe. Identify any clothes that are stained, torn or shabby. These can be recycled.

Items in good condition, but no longer worn, can be sent to a charity shop or sold to raise additional funds. Simply getting rid of these clothes will immediately shift your natural energy flow.

Buy yourself some new clothes or make a conscious decision to only wear the clothes that make you look and feel good. Remember that you deserve the best the Universe can offer.

Physical clearing is important because your body is your main tool for manifesting prosperity and abundance. Your body is a storehouse of memories; good and bad.

One of the best ways to clear physical clutter is exercise. I don't mean a gym session. Try dancing, drumming, chanting, jogging, swimming, walking, gardening, aerobic exercise or yoga.

Alternatively, you might like to try a reflexology treatment or have a massage. These are all good ways of physically clearing negative energy from your body. Sleep can also be a good way to physically heal and repair your body. Listen to your body. It will tell you what it needs.

There are two steps to successful physical clearing. The first step is doing something you can absorb yourself in. The second step is letting go and not dragging the memories back again. Releasing your memories is a conscious decision. If you insist on hanging onto unwelcome memories you're simply creating unnecessary clutter.

Whatever you choose to do allow yourself to be in the minute (also known as mindfulness). You might like to try the following Mindfulness Relaxation Technique Exercise.

Exercise: Mindfulness Relaxation Technique

Mindfulness is the ability to experience what you're doing currently without your mind filling with other thoughts. This technique may feel difficult to grasp initially but with practice everyone can master it. Mindfulness has long-term physical health and mental wellbeing benefits.

1. Choose a quiet place in your home, office, or garden etc where you can relax without distractions or interruptions

2. Get comfortable, but don't lie down as you may fall asleep. Sit on a chair or on the floor. Sit up with your spine straight. Alternatively, you can sit cross-legged or in the lotus position

3. Breathe in deeply through your nose and then exhale very slowly through your mouth

4. Repeat this breathing exercise for a couple of minutes until you feel yourself starting to relax

5. When you're relaxed and ready to start, choose a point of focus. This point can be internal (a feeling or imaginary scene) or something external. External items could include a picture, a flame or even a

meaningful word or phrase that you repeat throughout your session. You may meditate with eyes open or closed; the choice is yours

6. Keep breathing deeply, but now focus on your chosen object e.g. candle flame

7. Repeat this breathing and mindfulness until you feel ready to resume your normal activities. The longer you spend on this exercise the greater benefit your will experience

8. Sit quietly for a minute and notice how you're feeling. You should feel a sense of calm

9. Resume your normal activities

Note: It's important to adopt an observant, noncritical attitude. Don't worry about any distracting thoughts that go through your mind, and don't worry about how well you're doing.

If thoughts pop into your head during your relaxation session, don't fight them. Instead, acknowledge them, allow the thought to go and then gently turn your attention back to your point of focus.

Emotional Clearing

Emotional clearing can be the most painful type. It requires looking inwards and addressing the negative feelings you have about yourself and others.

The more critical and emotionally burdened you are the less prosperous you will feel. Conversely, the more loving, giving and forgiving you are the more prosperous you will feel.

Emotional clearing is anything you do that helps bring unpleasant feelings, emotions, stress or trauma to the surface. Then you can release and clear these emotions.

Meditation, reflective time, counselling etc can all be helpful for emotional clearing. The key to success is releasing the unpleasant feelings and emotions when they surface, not just suppressing them again.

Holding onto the pain from past relationships or people who have done you wrong is a form of emotional clutter. Although tempting to hold onto past hurts it actually takes a huge amount of energy not to forgive someone. By holding onto pain and anger you use up much-needed space for love in your heart and mind.

You need to allow yourself time to feel hurt and be angry, but don't hold onto it forever. When you're hurting shout, scream and cry, or do whatever else it takes to get the emotion out. Afterwards release the feelings and create some space for happiness in your life. Remember, you deserve happiness.

Holding onto past hurts may be tempting but it destroys you, not the person who hurt you. Forgiving simply means giving up the pain; it doesn't mean that you condone the behaviour that hurt you. A lot of refusing to forgive is about hurt pride more than anything else.

As you are what you think, the more love you send to yourself and others the more prosperous you will become on all levels.

It's natural to get angry, upset, jealous or resentful sometimes. You should never try to suppress these feelings but you do need to be able to release them in order to manifest true abundance. The sooner you can let go of negative emotions the sooner abundance can manifest.

Try focusing on the good in the person who is upsetting you. Otherwise, try the following positive affirmation "I'm sending you unconditional love, peace and happiness". In order to release the tension you need to mean what you're saying. Don't just pay lip service by simply uttering the words.

Forgiveness will enable the floodgates to prosperity and abundance to open for you. This will enable you to have the things you truly want in your life.

Spiritual Clearing

Spiritual clearing is about your aura (spiritual body). Your aura is the invisible and colourful energy field surrounding your outer body. This non-physical body extends three feet beyond your physical body. If your aura is blocked this will prevent you manifesting true prosperity and abundance.

Hurtful comments, feelings or experiences can create tension in your aura. These often manifest as apathy, indifference, lethargy, exhaustion or a negative mindset.

There are various ways of healing your aura. Reiki energy healing, colour healing, spending time enjoying nature or listening to ethereal music are all effective methods of spiritual clearing. It's important to practice spiritual clearing on a regular basis to ensure your soul is open to receiving Universal energy.

The following two exercises are designed to help you clear your emotional and spiritual clutter. A word of caution - you may find these exercises upsetting or emotionally draining. Just be kind to yourself.

In an ideal world you will always address issues immediately. For most of us this is not what actually happens. Instead we remember hurtful comments and actions for a long time.

Therefore, the first exercise deals with old hurts and emotional or spiritual clutter. The second exercise deals with new hurts and emotional or spiritual clutter.

Exercise: Releasing Past Hurts

These are feelings and emotions that you may have been suppressing for many years. Don't be surprised if you get upset during the releasing exercise.

1. Get a piece of paper and some blue or pink ink (the colour of the ink is important. Blue is the colour of communication and pink represents love)

2. Make a list of all the people who have hurt you in your life. This list is likely to be extensive and may take days, weeks or even months to complete

3. Choose one person from the list and write their name on a separate piece of paper

4. Next remember why you're so angry with that person, or how he/she hurt you

5. Feel the pain and hurt they have caused you. This might make you tearful. This is normal, but in order to move on you need to deal with this

6. Allow all your suppressed feelings to come to the surface. This could take anything from a few minutes to several days to complete

7. Write all your thoughts down

---

8. Only work on one person at a time. You need to release all the negative feelings you have about that person before you move onto the next person on your list

9. When your list is complete light a candle and hold the paper over the flame. Allow the paper to burn completely

10. As the paper burns visualise yourself letting go of past hurts caused by this person. These thoughts no longer serve a purpose in your life

11. Once you have released all the negative feelings, make a list of all the things that you once loved/liked about that person

12. Think of your happiest memories of the person. The list doesn't need to be extensive

13. This list of qualities or good points will help you to create a more balanced view of the person

14. Finally, complete the emotional healing process by saying "I forgive you and release you to the love of the Creator"

15. When you feel ready, move onto the next person on your list

Note: this exercise can be emotionally draining. Therefore, don't tackle more than one person on a single day. You may prefer to leave it for several days or weeks before you move onto the next person on your list.

If you're able to deal with new hurts, anger or jealousy immediately this will be much better for your physical, emotional and spiritual wellbeing. By releasing new hurts you will not be building up emotional clutter in future.

Exercise: Releasing New Hurts

1. When someone hurts you or makes you angry, jealous or resentful visualise that person. The clearer your image the better

2. Speak their name out loud or say it silently, whichever your prefer

3. Next, either silently or speaking out loud say the following mantra

"I now forgive you for............ [state what they have done]. I release you from my anger, jealousy, resentment (choose the emotion that applies). I bless you and all the good within you. I now affirm that both you and I are perfect, whole and complete, and we are one within the mind of the Creator"

4. Let go of the anger, hurt or resentment and move on. If you find yourself continuing to dwell on the person or hurt you have not cleared the emotions

In future, each time you feel deeply angry, critical, resentful or jealous repeat this exercise. The sooner the better!

If you regularly beat yourself up, or are overly critical of yourself, stop! You can use this exercise to forgive yourself as well as others. Whenever you feel tempted to harm yourself in this way repeat this exercise.

If you get into the habit of performing this exercise you will not have to deal with past hurts. You will find this exercise less painful than the releasing past hurts exercise.

In order to keep yourself free of physical, emotional and spiritual clutter:

1. Develop a positive attitude. Negativity is greater blocker to abundance

2. Learn to forgive yourself and others. You also need to be able to forget once you have forgiven

3. Release past experiences so they don't turn into emotional clutter. You're aiming to make experiences just a memory that you can recall from time to time

4. Release all bitterness, resentment and past grievances. This can be difficult if someone or something has caused you a great deal of pain. Unfortunately, holding onto the pain only harms your chances of future prosperity and abundance

5. Live your life in a way that matches your goals, values and desires

6. Learn to be grateful for everything you manifest, whether you did this consciously or unconsciously

"I've been getting rid of some clutter — anything that doesn't serve a positive purpose in my life — and making room for things that feel happy to me. Because I get to make my life whatever I want it to be.

I get to make the room feel however I want it to feel. I get to make the closet as full or as spacious as I want it. And, if I have more clutter to get rid of after Christmas, I'm not going to wait a year, or two or three to do it." Jan Denise (American Columnist, Author and Speaker)

5. Creating the Right Environment for Abundance

In the previous chapter I dealt with clutter and the impact this can have on your prosperity and abundance.

Once you have cleared your physical, emotional and spiritual blockages you can start to create the right environment for prosperity. If you are clutter free prosperity and abundance can flow freely.

Unfortunately, fear is another blocker to prosperity and abundance. Fear of failure or a subconscious belief that you're unworthy will simply put barriers in the way. Fear of success also hampers prosperity and abundance.

Not everyone is brave enough to admit they are frightened of success. Success means change. Sometimes the dream is all people really want. How much do you really want prosperity and abundance?

Prosperity and abundance happen naturally when you create the right environment. Your channels must be open. The energy must be able to flow freely, and you need to be receptive to what the Universe has to offer.

When abundance is not happening, something has gone wrong. Usually a consistent thought or belief has manifested itself as physical, spiritual or emotional clutter.

For a long time, metaphysicians have been telling us that thoughts can affect the world around us. Therefore, all you need to do is confront and release your self-limiting beliefs. This sounds simple but it can be difficult.

If you're currently experiencing poverty, on some level you must feel a conscious or subconscious need for this scarcity. You may have made the decision to accept this poverty before you came to earth. For some people, poverty is a life lesson they have to learn.

Poverty doesn't always mean lack of money. It can also relate to lack of material goods or emotional wellbeing. Poverty means something different to each of us.

Are you experiencing financial poverty, a loveless relationship, unemployment, or any other scarcity? If so, consciously or unconsciously you have chosen this for a reason. This might be because you don't feel worthy of abundance. It could even be a form or martyrdom. What are you getting from your scarcity?

Whatever has brought you to this point, it's your choice whether you stay in this state of poverty or open yourself up to prosperity and abundance. No one can make this decision for you, and no-one can create an abundant life for you. Only you can do this.

In order to change your life the first thing you need to do is address your self-limiting beliefs. Is your subconscious telling you that if you make lots of money your friends won't like you? Are you frightened that you won't fit in anymore? Are you frightened of falling deeply in love in case he/she decides to leave you?

One of the most remarkable things you can do for yourself is identify what your self-limiting beliefs are and do something about them. To really free yourself from your current poverty trap, you need to understand what you're getting from the current situation. Trust me, you are getting something.

This is a really tough conversation to have with yourself and should only be done when you feel emotionally strong enough to do so. Don't beat yourself up in your struggle to face up to these issues. Just know that when the time is right you will find the courage to tackle your self-limiting beliefs.

When you're ready to embrace prosperity and abundance, try the exercise below.

Exercise: What is Holding You Back?

It's absolutely essential that you're totally honest with yourself when doing this exercise. You don't need to share this information with anyone else, but complete honesty is the only way forward.

1. On a sheet of paper, create a table with three columns. The heading for column 1 is "Things I am dissatisfied with". The column 2 heading is "The reason for my dissatisfaction". The heading for column 3 is "What am I getting from the situation". Add as many rows as you need.

2. In column 1 make a list of all the things in your life that you're unhappy or dissatisfied with right now

3. This list may be long or short

4. Next to each thing on your list write an explanation about why you're dissatisfied in column 2

5. Now look at your list and ask yourself what you're getting from this situation. You must be getting something from it. See the explanation below. Write your answer in column 3

6. This exercise may take several days or weeks to complete as you need to really think about what is holding you back

7. When you have finished the exercise burn the paper. As it burns see yourself releasing all your self-limiting beliefs as they serve no purpose in your life. Know that you deserve prosperity and abundance

Be completely honest with yourself. You don't have to share this with anyone unless you choose to do so, but honesty is fundamental to success

Don't be self-critical or judgemental when creating this list. This will just hinder the process

My dissatisfaction and what I'm getting from it:
There are some common things people are often dissatisfied with. The list is not limited to these but includes - dissatisfaction at work, poor health, bad relationships and lack of money.

The reasons given are often things like I'm constantly passed over for promotion, every partner has left me for someone else, I'm always unwell, or I can barely exist on what I earn.

When you ask yourself the question "what am I getting from this situation" you may be surprised by the answer.

1. Perhaps you're scared of not living up to other people's expectations of you

2. Are you worrying about other people's opinion of you?

3. Are you frightened of success? For some success means they wouldn't have a goal any longer

4. Do you feel noble?

5. Does your situation make people feel sorry for you?

6. Does it stop you having to do things for yourself?

7. Does it save you from getting close to people?

8. Perhaps you get some excitement from the drama

9. Maybe you don't want to upset others or you don't want to assert yourself

The list of possibilities is endless, and the answers might be uncomfortable.

Identifying and addressing your self-limiting beliefs is the most challenging part of prosperity work. Give yourself a pat on the back for being brave enough to do it. From now on the route to prosperity and abundance will be much easier.

The next step is to recognise, and truly believe, that you're worthy of the best the Universe can offer. No matter what you have been told in the past believe that you are worthy. You deserve financial prosperity, love, good health, sense of wellbeing and anything else you desire.

Unless you genuinely believe that you're worthy you will never be able to manifest true prosperity and abundance. Anything is possible when you open yourself up to the power of the Universe.

It's important to be a friend to yourself. How can you expect others to be your 'friend' if you don't like yourself? Try the self-worth inventory exercise to see how your truly feel about yourself.

Exercise: Self-worth Inventory

Imagine looking at yourself as your friends see you. Next imagine describing this friend to someone who doesn't know you.

Make a list of all the good things about you. Your list should include physical characteristics, personality traits, talents, skills and accomplishments. I have listed some examples to start you off:

I have beautiful eyes

I have a genuine and spontaneous smile
I am kind and generous
I have achieved great career success
I was the first person in my family to go to University
I am multi-lingual
I play sport for the County or Country
I am a good and loyal friend

Make your list as thorough as possible. If you're struggling to do this think about what your family and friends might say about you.

Review your list regularly to remind yourself of just how worthy you are. As you think of new things you like about yourself, add them to your list. The more the better!

Hopefully you now understand what your family and friends like about you. Do this self-worth exercise anytime you're suffering with self-esteem issues.

Now you understand why you're worthy you can start to define what you want.

If you're new to prosperity work you may not instantly be able to define what you want to manifest. This is normal so don't beat yourself up about it.

Personally, I think it's helpful to stand back and think about your life currently. Is there anything you particularly want that you don't currently have? For example, a new job or relationship, a home of your own, start your own business etc.

Try the My Current Life exercise to help you to understand what has brought you to where you are right now. This will indicate what has helped shape you into the person you are today.

Exercise: My Current Life

1. On a blank sheet of paper, draw a circle. Divide your circle into eight equal segments. You will end up with something that looks like the spokes on a wheel

2. Write the following headings into the segments of your circle. Write one heading in each segment. It doesn't matter what order you do this in:

- Career
- Hobbies and interests
- Health and wellbeing
- Relationships
- Love and romance
- Personal development
- Money and finance
- Physical environment

3. This is called the 'Wheel of Life', which is a tool often used by life coaches. These headings represent the different aspects of your life

4. Look at your Wheel of Life, below, and think about the different parts of your life. Decide which aspects of your life you're happy with and which parts you're currently dissatisfied with

5. Score each aspect of your life in terms of how satisfied you are 1 = very dissatisfied (inner circle), 10 = very satisfied (outer circle).

6. Now, thinking about your life to date answer these questions:

a. Who are the people who have had a significant impact on your life (positive or negative)?

b. Which events have been significant in your life (positive or negative?

c. Do you have any regrets? If so, what are they? You may need to do the Releasing Past Hurts Exercise after answering this question

d. Are there any recurring themes in your life? (e.g. all relationships end in the same way)

e. What were your dreams and ambitions as a child?

f. Have you achieved them? If not, why not?

g. Which areas of your life are you least satisfied with?

h. Which areas of your life are you willing to change in order to reach complete satisfaction?

i. Which of your achievements mean most to you?

7. Review your 'current life' for at least a week, and amend it as necessary. Once you're satisfied that you have identified what you want to change you can set about it. Identify what will make you happy.

You can visualise achieving your goals. Alternatively, you may prefer to write a cosmic order or positive affirmations. The choice is yours.

It's important to clearly state what you want. Remember to state your requirements as if you already have what you want.

Release your request to the Universe and have complete faith that it will happen when the time is right. In order to achieve complete success your faith mustn't waiver.

The final step to creating the right environment for prosperity and abundance is to ensure you're open to receiving. This means being relaxed and allowing your inflow and outflow energy to move freely.

To do this I recommend you build meditation into your daily life. There are lots of different ways to meditate. You may need to experiment with several to find what works best for you.

I have tried many different meditations in the last 30 years. Currently I do a Transcendental Meditation (known as TM) for 20 minutes twice daily. You may find a different method that works for you.

"Abundance is not about waiting for something to happen. Abundance requires us to get into action to bring it into manifestation." Shamala Tan (Spiritual Coach)

Part Two

"Much effort, much prosperity" - Euripides

6. The Money Connection

Money is an energy form like any other. Money needs to continuously flow in order for you to generate true financial prosperity and abundance.

A negative attitude to money or limiting beliefs about money can cause an energy blockage. This is why it's important to develop a healthy relationship with money.

Let's be clear, money doesn't come to those who deserve it. Money comes to those who welcome it. Karmic issues (cause and effect) are something else, and not dealt with in this book. Your attitude to others with money affects your own prosperity.

Are you jealous of others with money?

Do you judge how wealthy they should be based on how they earn their money?

Do you judge whether they use their wealth wisely?

Do you believe wealthy people should be doing more to help others?

Do 'fat cats' make you angry?

Do you feel pangs of jealousy when you see people in nice cars, or wearing fabulous jewellery etc?

You may not feel comfortable answering these questions, but honesty is important if you want to move forward. You don't have to share your thoughts with anyone else but you do need to be honest with yourself.

If you have answered yes to these questions you have some serious issues with money. Your subconscious mind probably believes that others would have these thoughts about you if you were rich. This mindset will block true prosperity and abundance.

The Universe responds to the vibration i.e. money going where it's most welcome. If you have a negative attitude to money the Universe believes you wouldn't welcome money. The Universe then responds accordingly; it keeps money scarce.

If you would like more money or financial security you need to change the vibration, as like attracts like. Send the message to the Universe that you too would welcome money in your life. Start to enjoy and appreciate the money you have.

I'm not suggesting you squander what you have but enjoy spending it wisely. Don't be tempted to stockpile it as this will create an energy blockage eventually. There is no point being the richest person in the graveyard. If you stockpile your wealth and never enjoy or spend it, when you die it will be a hollow victory.

Think about the world's wealthiest people. Most share some of their wealth with worthwhile causes. You may think this is just because they can afford to. The reality is they choose to share it. They want to make the lives of others better too.

Each coin we put in a charity box is going to help someone else. Help doesn't need to be grand gestures that everyone notices. A small, sincere gesture can have a far greater impact on your prosperity and abundance. This is because it was given sincerely.

Keep telling yourself that money comes easily and frequently to you. This might feel like a lie to start with but keep plugging away until this mindset feels totally natural. We all have the ability to develop a positive attitude to money.

If you focus on lack and scarcity, you will attract more of what you don't have. With each bill you receive visualise receiving cheques to pay the bill. This tells the Universe that you will always have sufficient money to pay your bills. Bless each bill that you receive as it tells the Universe that someone thought you were worthy of credit.

People with issues around financial prosperity and abundance often say "I give; I give my time". This is the wrong type of giving if you're looking for financial abundance yourself. All you will get back from this kind of giving is other people giving you their time. This is probably not helpful if you're strapped for cash.

The best way to manifest financial abundance is to balance your giving. Ensure you give a combination of time, money and material goods. This will ensure a balance in what you receive.

You may ask for money and then feel disappointed when you don't get just what you asked for. For example, you may have asked the Universe to give you money to pay for professional advice. The Universe may arrange for this professional advice to be given to you free of charge.

Financial abundance doesn't always manifest itself as money. It may come in the form of goods or services that you don't have to pay for. Initially this may not feel like financial abundance.

If you're given the goods or services the money was needed for you have manifested financial abundance. Sometimes you have to use lateral thinking to recognise just what you have manifested. The Universe can be very subtle.

The Universe may not always be able to give you the exact sum you asked for but know that it will always try. The Universe can't perform miracles though. If you want to win the Lottery, buy a ticket! If you want a mortgage so you can buy a house, get a stable job.

If you want to create greater wealth, you first need to establish a healthy relationship with money. To get you started, try the following exercise:

Exercise: The Money Game

Imagine you have just been given the following sums of money. Visualise how you would spend each of these sums of money. Work through each amount in turn. Don't move on until you've answered the current question.

You may like to write your answers on a piece of paper. You may prefer to speak your answers out loud. Or, you may prefer to visualise your answers. The choice is yours.

1. If you were given £50 today how would you spend it?

2. If you were given £100 today how would you spend it?

3. If you were given £500 today how would you spend it?

4. If you were given £1000 today how would you spend it?

5. If you were given £10,000 today how would you spend it?

6. If you were given £50,000 today how would you spend it?

7. If you were given £1,000,000 today how would you spend it?

8. If you were given £1,000,000,000 today how would you spend it?

This exercise is designed to stretch your mind. It will increase your visualisation skills and help clarify what you would do with unlimited finances. You may like to do this exercise regularly to see how your desires change. You can then revise your goals accordingly.

Initially you may find it difficult to spend all this money. As you become more prosperous you will find the exercise gets easier.

Tithing is a historical practice that is often used in prosperity work to keep money energy flowing freely. Most religions expect people to tithe a percentage of their income to their place of worship. If you're not a religious person you may prefer to tithe to a different institution that helps you to feel closest to the Creator.

Tithe literally means tenth or 10%. A tenth of your income might feel like too much. If so, tithe a nominal sum instead. Then increase the amount as much as you want to or feel able to. The Universe will not judge you regarding the amount you give. It's the spirit of the giving that counts not the amount or frequency of your donation.

People who adopt the practice of tithing often make it their policy to tithe each time they get paid. Personally, I have been doing this for many years. Since I first adopted this practice I have seen a noticeable increase in my financial prosperity.

This is just my personal experience; not a recommendation that you should do the same. It's important to do what feels right for you.

Tithing is an excellent practice to help maintain the healthy balance of inflow and outflow energy. However, it's important to get the order of your tithing right. Most people get the order wrong.

They give to others first and spend only what is left (if any) on themselves. This tells the Universe that you come last in the pecking order. Break this habit now. The correct order for tithing is:

1. Give a percentage to a place of worship or institution that connects you to the Creator. You choose what percentage to donate

2. Give a percentage to yourself for celebration and treats

3. Use the remaining money to pay your bills, give to others or anything else you wish to do with it

You need to demonstrate to the Universe that you're setting funds aside for tithing. To do this physically separate the money you intend to use for your place of worship. You also need to set aside money for celebration or treats.

You can put these funds into pots, moneyboxes, piggybanks or a small chest/box set aside for this purpose. Clearly label your 'Creator' moneybox and your 'Celebration' moneybox to ensure they are not mistaken for something else.

Personally, I have a money jar for my 'Creator' tithes. Each year on the anniversary of my mum's passing I send the money collected to her church.

Although I'm not personally a religious person, this creates a win/win outcome. I demonstrate my gratitude to the Universe by sending funds to a place of worship. At the same time I recognise the anniversary of my mum's passing.

I also have a moneybox that I put money in for treats and celebrations. I put the same amount into both pots every time I earn, or win, some money. Then I pay my bills.

Terramundi pots have been used in Italy as a means of saving for celebration for the last 2000 years. Each pot is filled with coins or notes until the pot is full. When it's full the owner smashes the pot while making a secret wish.

It's customary to replace the Terramundi pot and start the process again. Giving to yourself sends an important message to the Universe about how you value yourself. The more you value yourself the more you will value others.

Make sure you always put something into your Creator and Celebration pots before paying your bills. You're sending a message to the Universe that you come before the bills.

This doesn't mean you should over indulge yourself and then not have enough for the bills. This would create bad karma. Prosperity and abundance always creates win/win outcomes.

I know this new way of thinking might feel uncomfortable especially if you don't currently have a lot of money. The money you put aside for you and the Creator can be a nominal sum. It's the intention not the amount that matters. As you become more prosperous you can increase the sum you put aside.

The miracle of tithing is you put 'the Creator' and yourself first, knowing there will always be enough money to pay the bills. If you pay the bills first, you're effectively neglecting yourself and this is the message you send to the Universe. This may result in just enough funds being available to pay the bills, leaving nothing for you.

Never tithe if you feel reluctant or resentful as this will be reflected in what you get back. By giving to 'the Creator', you're acknowledging 'that all things, including money, are due to the Creator's benevolence.

Karmic law says give willingly and you will receive abundance back. When you have very little money it may be difficult to spare funds for tithing. By sparing a little cash for tithing you will generate far greater prosperity and abundance in return.

Spending money is often misunderstood when talking about the outflowing of energy. Therefore, I thought I would tackle this issue before we go any further.

Some people are so addicted to spending that they dig themselves into financial holes. Others are so mean that they never share their good fortune and consequently people don't really want to be around them.

Neither attitude supports the healthy flow of inflowing and outflowing prosperity energy. Spending correctly can increase the inflow and outflow of prosperity energy. Like all energy, money needs to keep flowing. Don't take this as a recommendation to spend recklessly.

The golden rule is only spend what you can afford, but do it generously and without hesitation or apology. Above all "spend less than you have". Although this is common sense it's often ignored.

True abundance comes from within not by overspending, as this simply undermines any pleasure you felt. By overspending you're financing today's luxuries at the price of tomorrow's peace of mind.

Never give because you want to be loved. Also, give what is needed rather than what you want to give. If someone needs money giving your time will be of little benefit to them. It won't benefit you either.

Never do anything that makes you feel uncomfortable as this will not create abundance. A little resistance is normal when people are first introduced to prosperity work. This is different to being resentful or uncomfortable about giving. Resistance usually stems from having to demonstrate blind faith that what you give will be replaced with more.

It's bad karma to buy something that you really think you shouldn't buy. Never purchase an item that you feel guilty about buying as you will never feel true pleasure from it. The act of purchasing something that you feel unworthy of disrupts the natural flow of your prosperity energy.

It's important to get pleasure from every purchase. Each time you buy something, ask yourself "Is this something that will bring me joy?" Make a mental note of your total number of purchases in one week or one month. Calculate the number of purchases that gave you joy. If the number of purchases that gave you joy seems low, work on increasing this.

Be fair and reasonable when spending your money. Be willing to pay a fair price and never try to undercut someone just to get one-upmanship. Although many people like to haggle, it creates negative energy between you and the seller. This can be disruptive to your prosperity flow in the long run.

If you feel the need to haggle, ensure that you still end up paying a fair price for the goods. It's important that you both feel happy with the outcome.

It's impossible to be truly prosperous if you're trying to cheat someone else out of their prosperity. Prosperity and abundance will not come from stealing from someone else. That's not how prosperity and abundance works.

Although giving to charity is an important element of prosperity outflow, like all other spending it needs to be in balance. Never give more to charity or good causes than you can afford. No-one benefits when you become a martyr, but equally giving nothing will block your prosperity flow.

Only give to causes that you feel drawn to. Don't feel obliged to give to every good cause just because they asked for money.

If done for the right reasons, charitable giving circulates and redistributes prosperity and abundance. It also demonstrates to the Universe how you would like to be treated. Genuine charitable giving actually keeps your prosperity energy moving so that more can flow into your life.

I know this might require a huge leap of faith if you don't have a great deal right now. Start by giving small amounts of loose change to charitable causes. As your prosperity grows you can increase this to a more meaningful amount.

Exercise: Collecting Coins

The collecting coins exercise is a good way to tell the Universe you're open to receiving money from different sources.

1. Pick up any coins you find in the street and bless them. Don't just ignore them and walk on

2. If you only find coppers tell the Universe that you're grateful but start asking for silver coins in future

3. Either keep the coins or put them into a charity box

Note: some people believe that finding a coin in the street is a message from the Angels. Others believe once the coin is blessed you should pass it onto the next person you meet. This is believed to keep the goodwill flowing. It's fine to keep the coin or pass it on. The important bit is acknowledging it.

Make friends with money. Every time you handle a note or coin, bless it to cleanse it from any negative energy. Wonder about where it came from and how many people it has blessed on its route.

Bless it again as you release it to pay for something that you want. This will ensure that the money takes good energy on its forward journey.

We don't often write cheques these days but if you do, bless the cheques that you write. Write 'with thanks' on them after the amount instead of 'only'. On the back, write something like "every £1 I spend blesses the recipient and returns to me multiplied".

Bless your bills. Hold the bills in your hands and say "I bless these bills and know that I will be able to pay them easily and effortlessly". Or, say "I bless these bills, as I know that as I am sending money out, even more will come back to fill its place".

Remember, having bills to pay is a sign that someone thinks you're sufficiently prosperous for them to give you credit. Otherwise they would have asked for payment in advance. Tell the Universe that you're grateful for the trust placed in you.

Get to know the banknotes in your purse/wallet.

The £50 note has a picture of Matthew Boulton and James Watt

The new £20 note has a picture of Adam Smith

The £10 note has a hummingbird and Charles Darwin

The £5 note has a picture of Elizabeth Fry

Each of these people contributed something to mankind's development when they were alive.

Exercise: How Does it Feel to Have £1,000,000 or $1,000,000?

Here's another exercise that requires using your imagination. Imagine how it might feel to have £1,000,000 or $1,000,000.

1. In your search engine type "images of £1,000,000 banknote" or "$1,000,000 banknote"

2. Print the image. Hold the piece of paper in your hands, close your eyes, and imagine this is a real banknote

3. "What does it feel like to have one million pounds or one million dollars?" Spend five minutes thinking about this question. Think of the most positive, powerful, empowering and strong emotions and words you can come up with. The more conviction you put into your answers the greater the chance of making this a reality

4. Open your eyes and write your feelings down e.g. anything is possible, you feel free of financial worries, you're happy etc

5. Are you feeling more positive than before the exercise? If not, you may need to repeat the exercise. Allow your imagination to work its magic

6. It's important to remember this is a possibility. It can only become a reality if you allow it to turn into a reality

Bless your printed image of the £1,000,000 or $1,000,000 banknote regularly and watch your financial prosperity grow. It's only a piece of paper, but equally money is only energy. Dare to dream and enjoy the money you have. Remember, money goes where it is most welcome.

Money is meant to be a source of joy. The better relationship you can forge with money the easier it will be for you to accept prosperity and abundance.

Try the following affirmation "Money comes to me thick and fast from all directions, and I handle it beautifully". If you're seeking financial prosperity say this affirmation regularly and mean it. Remember to bless and appreciate all the money you receive, and share your good fortune.

"Your prosperity consciousness is not dependent on money. Your flow of money is dependent upon your prosperity consciousness." Louise L Hay

7. Cosmic Ordering

Cosmic ordering is not a new concept. It's been around for a very long time. Cosmic ordering is the name given to a version of positive thinking that was renamed by Barbel Mohr. Cosmic ordering is a term that is now widely used to describe the process of requesting and manifesting prosperity and abundance.

You can place your cosmic orders at any time of the day. Most people prefer to do this when they are alone, but not at a specific time. Furthermore, you don't need to be in a holy place to submit cosmic orders. The Universe (Cosmos) will pick up your vibration anywhere and at any time. It never stops working.

"With cosmic ordering you can keep your luxuries and ask for more." Stephen Richards (author of Cosmic Ordering: You Can Be Successful)

There are even an apps based on the philosophy of 'cosmic ordering'. They allow people to place orders with the Universe asking for their wishes to come true and then record what happens.

Like all prosperity work, there are some simple rules regarding cosmic ordering. Once you master these rules the sky is the limit, potentially.

1. You must know what you truly desire. If you don't know what you want how is the Universe supposed to know?

2. You must ask the Universe for it in a way that is clear and easily understood by the Universe

3. You must visualise what you want. The clearer the picture the greater the chance of success

4. You must truly believe that what you want is possible. This means a leap of faith and believing 100%

5. You must feel and behave as if you already have what you want. This strengthens the vibration

6. You must feel gratitude for what you want to manifest, as if you already have it

7. You have to protect your vision from non-believers. Be careful who you share your vision with as not everyone wants the best for you. Jealousy is a destructive energy

8. You must have total faith that your desires are coming to you. Doubt will prevent success

9. You must be open to receiving what you want. Be observant and notice when it happens

10. This must get into your subconscious programming

It's important that you believe that you're worthy of money, love, health, happiness and anything else you desire. Without this total belief you will not be able to manifest your greatest desires. The greater your belief the more prosperity and abundance you will manifest.

How is your body reacting to this statement? Are you smiling and nodding in agreement, or is your subconscious still resisting the change? If your subconscious mind has any doubts you will need to work on this before you can successfully manifest abundance.

Are you ready to create your first cosmic order? If so, try this exercise:

Exercise: Create a Cosmic Order

You can do this exercise wherever and whenever you like. You can do this somewhere private on your own, or work with a group of friends. You may like to make it a group activity so you can support and encourage each other. The choice is yours.

1. Relax completely. Start with a deep breathing exercise to get you into a relaxed state. When you're completely relaxed you will be able to think more creatively

2. Mentally decide what it is you truly want. This can be a single item or experience, or multiple things. Allow your thoughts to run loose in your mind. The more clearly you can visualise your desires the greater your chance of success

3. When you have a clear image in your mind write it down. Be as clear and specific as possible. Write your cosmic order as if you already have what you're asking for. Review your cosmic order to be sure it's correct

4. Now prioritise your wishes. Tell yourself and the Universe what is most important and what is least important on your list

5. Next, justify your cosmic order. What difference will it make to your life? What will you do with it, or as a result of it? Will anyone else, or the Universe, benefit too? This is just to test how important your request is to you

6. In order to create a strong enough vibration for manifestation the intention must be strong and focused. Do you truly believe you can have what you're asking for? Do you truly believe you're worthy of the best the Universe can offer? Without 100% commitment you either won't succeed or your success will be slowed down

7. Read your cosmic order out loud. Read it as if you are addressing a higher, much more powerful, authority. Think about how you would present your case to someone very important and influential. Treat your cosmic order in the same way

8. Place your cosmic order somewhere safe, but don't forget about it. Personally, I place mine under my pillow. This ensures my energy remains strongly connected to my cosmic order. Review it regularly, but not obsessively. Each time you review it, feel the success

Cosmic ordering beginners tend to be sceptical. I guess there's an element of "I don't want to make a fool of myself". If you don't try it you won't ever know how successful you could be.

If you're having doubts about cosmic ordering why not start with some small goals. Once you've tasted success you will want to go for bigger and bigger goals.

I like Jim Carey's story. I'm talking about Jim Carrey, the Canadian/American actor, comedian, and film producer.

Jim Carrey was a struggling young comedian trying to make it in Hollywood. He was ready to give up his dream of becoming a professional actor and comedian.

He had just performed at an open mic session at one of the nightclubs in Los Angeles. He was booed off the stage by his audience, and was feeling fairly down. He sat down, alone, at the top of Mulholland Drive and looked out at the city below.

He then pulled out his chequebook and wrote himself a cheque for $10 million. He wrote the following note on it: 'for acting services rendered.' This was his cosmic order to the Universe.

He then carried that cheque with him in his wallet everywhere he went from that day forward. By 1995 he was enjoying the success of Ace Ventura: Pet Detective, Dumb and Dumber, and The Mask. By this time his contract price had risen to $20 million.

Jim Carey created his cosmic order and believed in his success. He not only wanted this success, he took that leap of blind faith. That belief created such a strong vibration that the Universe more than delivered his request.

Imagine what you could achieve if you allow yourself to believe. I dare you to dream big and believe. I would love to hear from you when your dreams come true.

"With cosmic ordering it's not only your wealth that grows; your mind does too!" Stephen Richards

8. Working With Affirmations

Affirmations, are short, powerful statements that manifest the things you have in your life. You may be unconsciously using affirmations. This can result in things you don't want as well as things you do want.

Affirmations have an important role to play in prosperity work. They can be used to manifest what you want if you use them consciously.

Whether you say, think or hear affirmations they become thoughts. Thoughts, positive or negative, create a vibration. Each vibration connects the Universal consciousness with the Law of Attraction.

A passing thought doesn't normally manifest into anything tangible, but there are exceptions. For example have you ever thought of someone you have not seen for a while and within a few days they contact you or you bump into each other? This happened because the other person thought about you too. The vibration created by both of you was strong enough to manifest immediately.

Sometimes a single affirmation will create an outcome (positive or negative). On the whole affirmations need to be repeated regularly to make create a strong enough vibration. Only when the vibration is strong enough will something manifest.

Affirmations need to be repeated with attention, conviction and interest. The more you focus on something, good or bad, the sooner you will see the outcome.

Belief is the other key element when using affirmations to manifest prosperity and abundance. You need to truly believe that what you have asked for is going to manifest at the right time. Note: this may not be your desired timescale.

In order to manifest you need to believe that you are worthy of the best the Universe can give you. This is where self-limiting beliefs get in the way.

There is no 'right relationship' or 'right amount of money' that will ever give you a sense of self-worth. This is why you need to overcome any self-limiting beliefs. Until you do so you will never successfully manifest the sustainable prosperity and abundance you desire.

Some people believe that self-worth is earned through good deeds. This is wrong. Good deeds are nice but they will never give you a sense of self-worth. It's important that you learn to love yourself and overcome your self-limiting beliefs. Only then you will be on the way to prosperity and abundance.

Abundance operates on the Law of Attraction. The more you value yourself, the more you will attract the things and experiences that you value. Everyone has heard the expression 'money attracts money' – hence the Law of Attraction. If you already have money it's easy to attract more as your subconscious is already open to receiving it.

The same principle applies to everything else. Believing that you aren't worthy is like telling the Universe "send all the good stuff to someone else as I don't deserve it". You can't blame the Universe for responding to your request.

People often ask do positive affirmations work, and if so why do they work? The short answer is yes they do work.

Positive affirmations only work when they are translated into action. By conditioning your mind through positive affirmations, you clear out negative thoughts. This means that your dominant thoughts are of success, prosperity and abundance.

It's impossible to confirm how long you will have to say or think your positive affirmations before you manifest your wishes. Occasionally a single thought, e.g. thinking about someone you haven't seen for a while, will be sufficient. Sometimes affirmations will generate quick results and sometimes it may take years.

As a child I decided that I wanted to own a Volkswagen Beetle car one day. I even had a toy Volkswagen Beetle car. By the time I was old enough to drive the Beetle was out of production. I never forgot my childhood desire for a Volkswagen Beetle though. In fact I often told people about my childhood desire to own a Volkswagen Beetle.

Eventually Volkswagen launched the new Beetle and I was able to afford one. This affirmation manifested over 30 years after my original thought. I eventually owned three of them. You will be pleased to know most affirmations don't take this long to manifest.

Positive affirmations usually begin with "I am" or "I have". This is deliberate as it has a profound effect on the Law of Attraction. If you find yourself saying "I am fat, I am broke, or I am desperate and lonely" you will attract more of the same.

In the case of my Volkswagen Beetle car, I said "I'm going to buy a Beetle one day". I truly believed that one day I would own a Beetle car. Of course I had no idea the Beetle would be discontinued and then remanufactured.

When I was in a position to own a Beetle I had the means to purchase an original car or a new one. Fortunately for me, the Universe understood that I meant the car and not the insect.

It really is very important to ensure you're making positive statements that suggest you already have the things you're dreaming of. I didn't, which is probably why it took so many years to manifest my car. If my affirmation had been "I own a Volkswagen Beetle car" I would have got one much sooner.

You cannot change the past, so don't waste time focusing on lost opportunities or what ifs. Instead focus on the future, which you can influence. Sometimes opportunities appear for a brief moment. It's important to be aware and seize each opportunity when it appears. Opportunities won't wait for you.

If your main interest is work related start to think in terms of a fulfilling career. Visualise plenty of opportunities to do what you want. If you want a new job visualise yourself doing your dream job. Write and say positive affirmations that will bring the right job opportunity to you.

If you want to launch your own business, focus on it. Give your business a name. Define what your product offering is and how many clients you have etc.

Whether it's love, a bulging bank account, good health or anything else the rules are the same. First, visualise what you want. Next, write positive affirmations that tell the Universe you already have this.

If you are not sure exactly how to write effective affirmations here are a few pointers. Never say "when I have". This applies to time, money and material goods etc. You will never have these things if you word it this way. This simply tells the Universe it's wishful thinking, not a concrete goal.

Always state your desires as if you already have what you're asking for. Say things like "I'm playing a round of golf each week or I'm having golf lessons each week. I'm having a massage each week, I'm enjoying good health or I'm fit and healthy". Whether you want material goods or something less tangible the rules are the same.

It's good to write your own positive affirmations as this makes them very personal to you. In case you're struggling to get started here are some suggestions:

Health and Body Image Affirmations

I give thanks for health, happiness, prosperity and joy

Thank you for my healthy eyes, ears, nose, mouth, throat, heart etc. Name each part of your body

I am the healthiest I have ever been

I am in excellent physical and mental health

My health, strength and fitness are at optimum level

I look and feel great

I am perfectly healthy in body, mind and spirit

I love the way I feel when I take good care of myself

I radiate good health

I am growing more beautiful day by day

Today I choose to honour my beauty, my strength and my uniqueness

Relationship Affirmations

I have released fear and opened my heart to true love, which is what I now have

I am ready for, and enjoying, a healthy, loving relationship

I am the perfect partner for my perfect partner

I am very happy and grateful that [name] and I found each other. We have a very blessed relationship

I am living my perfect life with my perfect partner, who is a friend, lover and soul mate

Thank you Universe for bringing [name] into my life. My life is now complete with this beautiful human being

All of my relationships are meaningful and fulfilling

I am grateful for all the lovely people in my life

I deserve the loving and healthy relationship I have

The Universe has already introduced me to my perfect partner

I am surrounded by very lovely and genuine friends

Financial Affirmations

I ask that everyone who receives blessings from my products/services be given the money they need to purchase them

I give thanks for a quick and substantial increase in my financial income now

My income is constantly increasing and I prosper wherever I turn

I am willing to be prosperous no matter what other people think

I have plenty of money. It comes to me easily and effortlessly

Money and success come to me easily

I make plenty of money doing what I love

Money flows to me from all directions easily and effortlessly

My financial situation is wonderful. I have absolute confidence in my ability to generate any income I choose

My business has an annual turnover of [sum]

I have plenty of money to share

I am happy to share my wealth and good fortune with others

I am happy to share my financial prosperity with others

Career Affirmations

I have plenty of opportunities to have the career I want

I now have plenty of career opportunities to enable me to achieve whatever I want

I'm doing the job I love, and am being richly rewarded for it

I will pass my annual appraisal with flying colours

I respect my abilities and always work to my full potential

I am a great business leader

I have fulfilled my ambition to start and run my own business

I am running my own very successful business

Abundance and Prosperity Affirmations

I am open to the flow of great abundance in all areas of my life

I always have more than enough of everything I need

Thank you, thank you, thank you, thank you Universe!

I am always directed to the people who need what I have to offer

Prosperity surrounds me, prosperity fills me, and prosperity flows to me and through me

I am willing to experience all the wealth and joy the Universe has for me now

I bless and appreciate all that I have and look with wonder as it increases

Thank you for this wonderful abundant world

I open my mind to abundance

White light surrounds my house. Thank you angels for sending an appropriate angel to protect it

I am prosperous and fulfilled

I have all that I desire. It comes to me easily and effortlessly

Thank you Universe for giving me this abundant life

Life Purpose Affirmations

I am what I am and that's ok

I accept others as they are

Joy, joy, joy. I lovingly allow joy to flow through my mind, body and experiences

I will die peacefully and easily when the time is right for me

All things are possible through the divine spirit within me

I am limited only by my vision of what is possible

Angels of prosperity walk with me, work with me wherever I am, whatever I see

I am worthy of the best that the Universe can offer

I am willing to forgive. I am willing to release everything that blocks my prosperity and abundance

I am willing to live a simpler, happier and more prosperous life

My life purpose can be whatever I decide to make it

I have let go of worn out thoughts, worn out relationships and worn out conditions. Divine order is now established and maintained in me and in my world

I am willing to receive all the good and abundance the Universe has for me now

I am open and receptive to all the good and the abundance that the Universe has for me now

I am a channel for Universal prosperity and abundance

I am worthy of the best the Universe can offer

I am more than good enough

I have plenty of opportunities to live the life I want

My life is filled with prosperity on all levels

Self-love Affirmations

I am filled with light, love and peace

I'm proud of all that I have achieved

I love myself no matter what

I treat myself with kindness and respect

You can create positive affirmations for any area of your life e.g. health, finances, career, relationships, spirituality, personal growth or self-esteem etc.

Are you ready to have a go at writing your own affirmations?

Exercise: Writing Affirmations

Writing affirmations is a deeply personal and powerful exercise. The aim is to write a statement that generates your target feeling. You can write as many affirmations as you like. The Universe doesn't set a limit on how much you can ask for.

1. Decide what you want. Is it better health, gain a better figure, increased prosperity, a new job etc? Think about how you will feel when you achieve this

2. Make sure your affirmations are positive, written in the present tense and personal to you. Use words like "I have..., I receive..., I am..."

3. Make sure you write your affirmations in your natural speaking style. This will feel more natural when you read them

4. Write short affirmations that you can remember

5. Include words that convey positive feelings e.g. "It's fantastic that..., I'm so happy that...., I'm delighted to......."

6. Affirmations must be believable. If you feel uncomfortable then it's not the right affirmation for you

7. As the Universe works on the Law of Attraction it gives you more of what it thinks you already have. This makes your choice of words very important

8. Don't set a timeline. Trust the process to work when the time is right

Remember, the stronger your belief the stronger the vibration. The stronger the vibration the sooner you will manifest your wishes. Dare to dream and believe.

"If you can imagine it, you can achieve it. If you can dream it, you can become it." William Arthur Ward (author of Fountains of Faith)

9. Colour and Prosperity

Colour is a fundamental building block for visualisation. It's closely associated with your mental and emotional states, and can affect them profoundly.

"Colour is a power that directly influences the soul." Wassily Kandinsky (Russian painter)

The seven colours in the rainbow correspond with the mystical number seven. It's also the number of major chakras in the human body. Wherever you are and whatever you're doing, colour is always with you. Sometimes you may be more conscious of it than at other times.

Different colours are often used as shorthand to describe emotional states, gender or political status. In the English language colour is often used to describe states of feeling. For example - 'in the pink', 'green with envy', 'feeling blue', 'in a black mood', 'seeing red', or 'off colour'. Here in the UK, each political party is associated with a colour.

The more you're aware of colour the more likely you are to dream in colour. You may respond to some colours in a very personal way. For example - some colours will make you feel happy or energise you, while other colours make you feel depressed.

Some colours will have a cultural association for you. For example - in western culture brides wear white on their wedding day. In eastern culture white is worn for funerals. In Chinese culture red symbolises good fortune and joy.

Colour therapy (chromotherapy) should not be something you just go to a therapist to 'have done to you'. Colour is everywhere and should be utilised as part of your everyday life.

Traditionally brown, green and gold are associated with prosperity work, but all colours can be used for prosperity work.

The use of colour is a truly holistic, non-invasive and powerful therapy which dates back thousands of years. Colour therapy can be used for any problem whether, physical, mental, emotional or spiritual. Colour therapy can also be used for specific problems, or as an overall relaxation therapy.

Being aware of your colour preferences can tell you a great deal about yourself. It can help you to address deep seated emotional issues, character traits etc. Colour can be incredibly enlightening and transforming.

Learn to listen to your body. You will be intuitively drawn to the colours your physical, emotional or spiritual body needs at that time. For instance, you may feel the need to wear red. This is usually because you need an energy or confidence boost.

Working with the appropriate colour/colours can help to dispel negative feelings. It can also free energy blocks and re-balance your body.

You can wear colour to help influence your prosperity and abundance or consciously build colour into your surroundings. Both methods work well.

Here's a summary of the most common colours and their benefits.

Black – provides comfort while protecting your emotions and feelings, and hiding vulnerabilities, insecurities and lack of self-confidence. For prosperity work, use black to break up old ways of doing things and create major change in your life. Black is great for banishing poverty and debts. If you need an emotional comfort blanket, wear black.

Blue – has many purposes. It's associated with peace, calm, wisdom, spirituality and communication. It's a good colour to wear during difficult times. Blue can provide inspiration if you are writing books or articles, studying, delivering presentations or public speaking. Blue is also considered to be a healing colour. If you need a little TLC wear blue.

Brown – is a wonderful prosperity colour. On one side it's grounding; providing stability, structure and support. On the other side it's great for attracting money or material goods (e.g. a new home etc). If you have difficulty managing your finances or keeping a job brown is a good colour for you.

Brown is also an excellent colour to wear if you feel disconnected in any way. It's a great stabiliser. Balance brown with a more vibrant colour so you don't become too grounded to enjoy life.

Burgundy - can be used to stimulate inspiration in business dealings. Burgundy can also be used to attract money or material comforts into your life. If burgundy is your colour choice, you are ready to take charge of your situation.

Gold – is the colour that rules prosperity and abundance. In a nutshell, gold is viewed as the colour of success, achievement, triumph, prosperity, luxury, quality, prestige and sophistication. Gold is a feel good colour that can be beneficial for any kind of prosperity work. If you can't make up your mind which colour you're most drawn to, opt for gold. Incorporate a little gold into your life. It won't let you down. Gold is a good background colour for prosperity wheels (vision boards).

Green – is a traditional prosperity colour. It's associated with good fortune, growth, wealth, fertility, new beginnings and health. Use green only for increase. Never use green if your affirmations are about ridding yourself of anything e.g. debt. Green is an excellent colour to use if you want to draw more money into your life.

Grey – is perceived to be an unemotional, solid and stable colour. It's a useful colour for adding depth and seriousness to your prosperity work. It's also helpful for unlocking the knowledge about yourself that is necessary to truly manifest prosperity. Use grey to create a balance between physical and non-physical forms of abundance. Like brown, grey needs to be balanced with more vibrant colours.

Indigo - is the colour of intuition and perception. This deep midnight blue promotes deep concentration during times of introspection and meditation. It will help you to achieve deeper levels of consciousness. Indigo stimulates the right brain. It's useful for prosperity work as creativity is a key part of manifesting abundance.

Lavender – a blend of purple and white (two very good colours for prosperity work). Lavender is associated with meditation, spiritual protection, success and blessings. Wear lavender when you want to attune your prosperity goals with your spiritual beliefs. Lavender is also associated with all forms of healing and wellbeing.

Magenta – is a deep red with some purple in it, so can raise your energy level. Use magenta to make your prosperity work proceed quickly. Wear magenta if you want to ensure success in matters of the highest importance. A little magenta can go a long way.

Orange – is another colour traditionally associated with abundance and prosperity. It also represents enthusiasm, success and creativity. It's a great for banishing repression. Orange is a good prosperity colour as it works quickly. Orange is a perfect networking colour as it gets people talking and thinking. Use orange in moderation as it's such an 'in your face' colour.

Peach – is a combination or orange and white, it represents the purest form of prosperity. Use peach to keep your mind focused on prosperity or forging deep friendships. Wearing the colour peach directs your energy towards others in a loving and caring way. It's a soothing and comforting colour.

Pink – is the colour most often associated with love, friendship, emotional healing, nurturing, compassion and security. Use pink in all prosperity issues involving close family or friends. There is no better colour for emotional prosperity than pink as it is both soothing and offers hope. Any shade of pink will do, so choose the shade that's right for you.

Red – represents energy, strength, courage and willpower. It's also associated with inspiration, sexual desire and romantic love. Wear red whenever you need courage or need to draw in extra inspiration.

Red, like orange, tends to create dramatic change quickly. Wear red for protection when you think your prosperity is being threatened by an outside source.

The good news is red suits everyone. You will need to choose the right shade of red for you, but there is one for everyone.

Silver – is a soothing, calming and purifying colour. Silver signifies a time of reflection or change of direction as it illuminates the way forward and creates a reflection.

Silver helps with cleansing and releasing mental, physical and emotional issues and blockages. It opens new doors and lights the way to the future. This is a good background colour for prosperity wheels (vision boards).

Turquoise – recharges your spirits during times of mental stress and tiredness. Turquoise is an ideal colour for prosperity work as it can heal the emotions and create emotional balance. Turquoise can be used to stimulate communication and clarity, or when a situation requires great patience. Use it with gold or silver to win success in business.

Violet (Purple) – is a combination of red and blue. It's used in colour therapy for detoxification due to its intense purification properties. Scarlet raises the blood pressure while blue lowers the blood pressure. Violet is associated with success of all kinds. This includes psychic powers, spirituality and protection, making it an excellent colour for all prosperity work.

White – is symbolic of clarity, purity, protection and freshness. Wearing white helps to cleanse the mind and develop spiritual understanding. It really needs to be a clean, bright white because once it gets dingy and dull your emotions can mirror the dullness.

White is a safe colour to use for all prosperity work. It's the purest form of energy. If you see white during your meditation you are forming a strong link with the spirit world.

Yellow – is seen as a sunny and cheerful colour. It resonates with the left (logical) side of your brain. As yellow is good at creating mental agility wear it whenever you need to sign contracts or negotiate payments. When your prosperity depends on persuading someone to your way of thinking, choose yellow.

Colour Preferences

Many studies have been carried out over the last century on colour preferences. This has confirmed that we all have personal colour preferences.

Research has confirmed that most people are drawn to cooler colours. These are the hues of blue and green. Research also suggests that people tend to like brighter and more colourful colours. Dark and less colourful colours aren't as popular.

Colour preferences are deeply rooted emotional responses that appear to lack any rational basis. Some believe our colour preferences are based on the following:

A life experience involving a particular colour may influence your choice. A negative life experience involving a particular colour will make you dislike a certain colour. Equally, a positive life experience involving a particular colour will make you feel drawn to that colour

You may be drawn to a colour as you have an imbalance in that particular area of your body. This is explained more under the Chakras heading.

You don't need to wear colours as outer garments. You may choose to wear your colours as lingerie, a ribbon or jewellery. You may prefer to use your colour preferences in your physical environment.

Chakras

What are chakras? Around your physical body there is an auric energy field, known as the aura or subtle body. This energy field interacts with your physical body through spiralling energetic forces known as chakras.

Each chakra in your body is an energy centre. There are seven of these major energy centres in your body. All energy flows through our chakra energy centres. Physical, emotional or spiritual ill health occurs when one or more chakra is blocked.

Each chakra links to your spiritual, physical, emotional, or mental body. The chakras are the network through which the mind, body, and spirit interact as one holistic system. In order to manifest unlimited abundance your chakras need to be balanced.

The subject of chakras is extensive. This topic could fill an entire book. Therefore, I have limited my comments about chakras to prosperity and abundance. If you wish to know more about chakras you can find plenty of information available on the internet.

Each chakra is influenced by a specific colour and is associated with specific parts of your physical body. Each chakra has its own individual characteristics and functions. Your chakras are also linked to one of the seven colours of the rainbow spectrum.

Your ability to successfully manifest what you want will be increased if your chakras are balanced.

The chakras run up the centre of your body from the base of your spine to your crown. I have included a brief summary of each chakra. Please don't assume this is all there is to know about chakras.

Base (Root) Chakra
The base chakra is located in the tailbone of your spine. Red is the colour of this chakra.

The base chakra represents your foundation and feeling of being grounded. This chakra is associated with your bones, teeth, nails, gonads, anus, rectum, colon, prostate gland, blood and blood cells.

Sacral Chakra
The sacral chakra is located in your lower abdomen. It's about two inches below the navel and two inches in. Orange is the colour of this chakra.

The sacral chakra is associated with your pelvis, kidneys, adrenalin, bladder, blood, lymph, gastric juices and sperm. This chakra represents your connection and ability to accept others and new experiences.

Solar Plexus
The solar plexus is located in your upper abdomen in the stomach area. Yellow is the colour of this chakra.

The solar plexus chakra represents your ability to be confident and in-control of your life. This is why we are encouraged to focus on our solar plexus if we're feeling nervous. This chakra is also associated with your lower back, digestive system, liver, spleen, gall bladder, pancreas and insulin.

Heart Chakra
The heart chakra is located in the centre of your chest slightly to the right of your physical heart. This chakra is associated with two colours. Green or rose pink is the colour of this chakra.

The heart chakra represents your ability to love and feel compassion. This chakra is important if love is one of your aspirations. This chakra is associated with your heart, upper back, lungs, and blood and air circulation.

Throat Chakra

The throat chakra is located in your throat, between the collar bones. Turquoise or sky blue is the colour of this chakra.

Your throat chakra represents your ability to communicate effectively. It's associated with all forms of communication. This chakra is also associated with your windpipe, throat, neck, thyroid, parathyroid gland, and ears.

Third Eye (Brow) Chakra

The third eye chakra is located on your forehead between your eyebrows. Indigo is the colour of this chakra.

The third eye chakra represents your ability to focus on, and see, the big picture. This chakra is also associated with your face, nose, sinuses, ears, eyes and brain functions.

Crown Chakra

The crown chakra is located at the very top of your head. Violet is the colour of this chakra. Some people say this chakra is influenced by white or gold, but generally violet is the colour associated with the crown chakra.

The crown chakra represents your ability to be fully connected spiritually. This chakra is associated with your cerebrum and pineal gland; thus affecting your entire body. This chakra is important in prosperity work.

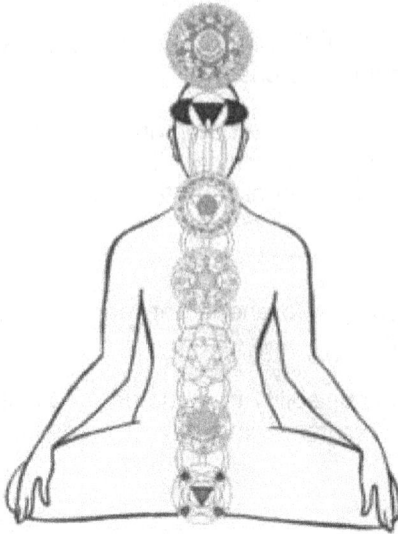

Crown - Spiritual

3rd Eye - Perception

Throat - Expression

Heart - Love

Solar Plexus - Power

Sacral - Sex

Root - Survival

The following exercise is designed to help you understand the state of your chakras currently.

Exercise: Sensing Your Chakra Energies

You can do this exercise as often as you like. You may even like to record the results so you can monitor any changes. This exercise is a form of meditation.

1. Find a quiet place where you can relax. Close your eyes and start to breathe in deeply through your nose and then slowly exhale (breathe out)

2. Repeat this for at least 5 minutes. With each breath feel your body and mind beginning to relax

3. Now start to sense your body and your aura. Release any emotions that you become aware of during this mediation

4. You are simply sensing how your unique energies are flowing at present. Don't make any judgements

5. Check from your feet up to your head and notice any clues your body is giving you

6. When you feel ready open your eyes. Now, without thinking, identify any colours you saw when you did this exercise

Note: there are no right or wrong answers to this exercise; it's merely your observation of your aura. Below is an interpretation of your body image.

You may have sensed a good balance of colour throughout your body. Or, you may have just sensed blocks of colour in a particular part of your body. Initially you may not sense anything at all, but this will come with practice.

Red represents, vitality or anger. Dull red in your aura may represent ill health

Pink indicates unconditional love. However, excessive pink in your aura may indicate that you are not grounded right now

Orange represents joyfulness and balanced sexuality. Excessive orange suggests an imbalance in your aura

Gold or golden yellow indicates joy, intellect or mental processes. This suggests you are mentally alert. Too much gold or golden yellow may suggest hyperactivity

Lemon yellow suggests you are feeling vitriolic, or have a defensive attitude. Yellow can also represent change. Be observant and see what unfolds in the coming days or weeks

Green suggests balance, peace and harmony. However, dark green is a sign of moodiness, intransigence or ill health

Turquoise blue is a very positive and balanced colour to sense when you do this exercise

Bright blue is also a very positive and balanced colour

Indigo below the level of your heart suggests a heavy personality. If you sense indigo above the level of your heart it suggests you are a dreamer, thinker or meditator. If you sensed indigo in your aura then it suggests you may be feeling sluggish. Wear an uplifting colour to balance your system

Violet or purple below the level of your heart suggests you are not currently grounded. If you sense violet or purple above your heart or in your aura it suggests spiritual development. If you're open minded it will take you on an interesting journey

Magenta indicates a visionary spirit. However, if you sensed an excessive amount of magenta during this exercise you are not currently grounded. You might like to try some grounding exercises to return to a balanced state

Black in small quantities in your aura suggests that you are not very well. Don't panic, this isn't necessarily serious. If you sense black at your feet it suggests you are grounded. Large areas of black in your body usually suggest depression, repressed anger, dominance or addictions

Grey suggests authority or control, but it can also indicate repression. If you sensed grey in your aura you may be unwell. A lighter shade of grey may suggest you feel comfortably in control of your life

Brown is generally thought to be a good colour as it suggests you're grounded. When doing this exercise black and brown may look very similar so it could be either of these colours.

Note: If you observed yellow during this meditation reflect on the shade of yellow you experienced.

The more peaceful and balanced you feel the easier it will be for you to manifest prosperity and abundance. Self-limiting beliefs are one of the greatest inhibitors to prosperity and abundance. Self-limiting beliefs may manifest in the colours you saw when you did this exercise.

Although I have already included an exercise to help deal with your self-limiting beliefs, here is another one that you may like to try:

Exercise: Releasing Negative Patterns

1. Find a quiet place where you can relax. Breathe in deeply through your nose and then slowly exhale (breathe out)

2. Repeat this deep breathing for a couple of minutes. Use this time to release any thoughts running through your mind. Don't judge your thoughts, just allow them to come and go

3. When your mind is still, read each of the following statements. Select the statement that reflects your position now. Be honest with yourself

4. Count the number of times you have circled 'No' and read the analysis at the end of the exercise

I can relax easily (Yes/No/Sometimes)

I feel comfortable in my own body (Yes/No/Sometimes)

I can use my mind creatively (Yes/No/Sometimes)

I feel comfortable with spiritual concepts (Yes/No/Sometimes)

I enjoy my own company and am happy to be alone (Yes/No/Sometimes)

I enjoy the company of others (Yes/No/Sometimes)

I try not to judge people by their appearance (Yes/No/Sometimes)

I have an open mind (Yes/No/Sometimes)

I have a good memory (Yes/No/Sometimes)

I find it easy to concentrate (Yes/No/Sometimes)

I take good care of my body (Yes/No/Sometimes)

I appreciate my family, friends and my home (Yes/No/Sometimes)

I enjoy helping other people (Yes/No/Sometimes)

I have a postive self-image (Yes/No/Sometimes)

I see the best in all situations (Yes/No/Sometimes)

I have useful premonitions (Yes/No/Sometimes)

I find it easy to go to sleep (Yes/No/Sometimes)

I have colourful and exciting dreams (Yes/No/Sometimes)

I find it easy to visualise things (Yes/No/Sometimes)

I appreciate and enjoy being in nature (Yes/No/Sometimes)

I meditate regularly (Yes/No/Sometimes)

If you answered 'No' to any of these statements you are holding some unhelpful patterns in your chakras or aura.

If you answered 'No' to 5-10 of these statements you need to work on these aspects. Read each statement where you selected 'No'. Next, decide what changes you are going to make.

If you answered 'No' to more than 10 of these statements you are holding some seriously unhelpful patterns. If you don't address these negative patterns it will ultimately affect your physical health. Aside from that, you're making it very difficult to manifest prosperity and abundance.

Think about how you can remedy your negative patterns and create an action plan for yourself. It's important to review your action plan regularly to see if you are making progress towards a balanced state.

There is now an app 'Relax & Chromotherapy' if you want a relaxing tool with you at all times. This is available on Google Play Store.

Of course chakra balancing isn't the only way to incorporate colour into your life. The easiest way to make colour a conscious part of your life is through the clothes you wear. Listen to your body, it will tell you which colours to wear.

If you want to use colour to manifest prosperity and abundance into your life, any of the following will work:

Wear clothes or jewellery in the colours you feel drawn to

Eat food in the colours your body needs

Write or draw with coloured pens or crayons. You can used coloured gel pens for writing notes at home and at work

Decorate with colour

Paint with colour. It may bring out your hidden artistic talents

Use colour in prosperity spells. You can use your search engine to find prosperity spells

Use coloured paper or card for your prosperity wheel (vision board) or cosmic orders

Buy or grow flowers in your chosen colours

Burn a candle in the appropriate colour

Visualise yourself surrounded in a bubble of your favourite colour. See this bubble protecting and healing you

"Your attitude is like a box of crayons that colour your world. Constantly colour your picture grey and your picture will always be bleak. Try adding

some bright colours to the picture, and your picture begins to lighten up."
Allen Klein (founder of ABKCO Music and Records)

10. Prosperity Crystals

Crystals have been used for centuries in prosperity work. Each crystal is a form of energy. Crystals emit tiny electrical impulses, which are received and recognised by your body's neurological system. Crystals release energy blockages in your body and increase the vibration.

It's believed that having a large crystal in a room can help reduce negative energies and harmonise imbalanced energy patterns. Personally, I keep a large amethyst in my study and one under the bed.

There are over 4,000 crystals in the world so it's no, surprise that some have a part to play in prosperity work. Any green, gold or earth coloured stones can be used to manifest prosperity and abundance. Other colours work too, as they work on different parts of your body.

With over 4,000 crystals in the world I can't possibly cover the subject extensively. I have selected the crystals most commonly associated with prosperity work. You may find other crystals that you prefer to work with.

Every crystal has its own energy and benefits so it's worth understanding how each crystal can be used. Below I have listed my recommendations and their benefits.

Choosing crystals is a very personal experience. The stone that feels right for you may have no impact on somebody else. Therefore, if possible each person should select their own crystals.

Later in this chapter I have suggested how you might use your crystals in your prosperity work. First, let's look at the crystals themselves:

Agate: is available in blue, white, grey, brown, red, green, yellow, black and rose. Agate is excellent for rebalancing and harmonising your mind, body and spirit. Agate encourages clear, rational and analytical thinking, which is useful for cosmic ordering.

Amazonite: is a beautiful turquoise, blue-green colour, often found with white or grey sections. Amazonite balances your Yin and Yang, and opens your heart and throat chakras. It's a good stone for connecting you with your own inner power, which is necessary for successful manifesting.

Amber: is a transparent or translucent fossilised tree resin. It can range in colour from dark brown to a light lemon yellow. Amber is used to promote good luck, happiness, success and increase confidence, which is why it's useful for prosperity work.

Amethyst: is a purple coloured variety of quartz crystal. Amethyst comes in shades from deepest violet to pale lilac and white. Amethyst is used because of its power to influence your subconscious mind and balance your physical, mental, emotional and spiritual aspects. It's a very lovely stone to have as it helps create a sense of balance, patience and peace.

Ametrine: is a mixture of the purple amethyst and yellow Citrine, and has the healing powers of both. Ametrine is good for dissolving emotional blockages and easing transition for prosperity work. It can be very useful when changing job or partner.

Angelite: is an opaque, blue and white crystal that sometimes contains flecks of red. Angelite is good for healing anger and aiding communication. It also promotes feelings of peace and tranquility. You might find this crystal useful if you choose to do the Healing Past Hurts exercise.

Aquamarine: ranges from a light sky to the deep blue of the sea. Aquamarines encourage you to express your emotions and give you confidence to face up to situations. In terms of prosperity work aquamarines aid communication (with the Universe or people).

Aventurine: ranges from blue, blue-green, brownish-red, grey to yellow. The most common colour, however, is green. It encourages feelings of deep relaxation and contentment.

This is an excellent crystal if you feel unloved or find it difficult to open up your heart to trust and form relationships with others. If your ambitions are focused on a new or better relationship an Aventurine may help.

Calcite: is found in blue, green, orange, pink, red and black. It can also be colourless. Calcite is a great stone for students as it amplifies learning abilities. This can be helpful if one of your aspirations is around learning, exam success or developing skills for a new role.

Carnelian: is most commonly found as orange-brown, brown, red, red-brown or pink crystals. It's good for banishing negative energy. A carnelian is also good for recovery after rejection as it eliminates feelings of inadequacy and low self-worth. Overcoming your self-worth issues will help prosperity and abundance to manifest for you.

Chrysocolla: is usually a bright blue-green colour, although it can be brown or black. Chrysocolla is a great balancer. The calmer and more balanced you are the easier it will be to manifest prosperity and abundance.

Citrine: is golden-yellow coloured. It's renowned as one of the most powerful healing stones. Citrine is great for stimulating your brain and strengthening your intellect. It also promotes new ideas and creativity. Citrine is also recognised as a stone of abundance and prosperity. I recommend everyone has a Citrine.

Clear Quartz: is the most common mineral on the planet. It's often known as 'the bones of Mother Earth'. Quartz is a 'communication crystal'. It's able to absorb, focus and transmit energy, making this a very useful crystal for prosperity work.

Emerald: is a bright green stone, often known as the stone of love. Emeralds are good for promoting harmony and wholeness in every aspect of your life. It's a very useful stone for prosperity work.

Flint: is a very hard but brittle grey or black coloured stone. It can be used to banish anything that you want to remove from your life.

Although this book focuses on manifesting prosperity and abundance sometimes you need to clear things from the past in order to move forward. Flint will help you do this.

Fluorite: is found in a variety of colours including white, pink, magenta, purple, black, blue, green and yellow. Fluorite is a good meditation stone. It can help you to understand that you are in the most ideal place you could ever be in. This positive attitude helps with prosperity work.

Garnet: ranges in colour from shades of red, brown, black, orange and green. It derives its name from 'pomegranate'. Garnets keep you grounded, and can be used to stimulate creativity and bring commercial success. A garnet is a very useful if your aspirations are business related.

Haematite: is an iron gemstone with a beautiful metallic sheen and natural magnetic properties. It's used to break through any barriers that may be holding you back from achieving what you want. It's especially good for dealing with fear, inhibition, guilt, worry or self-doubt. Haematite is a useful stone in getting you to the point you are ready to start manifesting.

Jade: can take on any shade from creamy white through to deepest green, purple, yellow and black. Jade can be used to break the unwanted links that bind you to people or places that no longer serve you. Jade is a useful stone if you are seeking financial prosperity.

Jasper: can be found in a variety of colours. Orange, brown, green, yellow and red are the most common. Jaspers can be used to enhance your spiritual connection to Earth or for emotional balance. If your aspirations are spiritual or emotional you might like to have a piece of Jasper.

Jet: is fossilised organic substance, similar to coal. Jet is said to be helpful for anyone who finds it hard to make decisions or to say 'no' when they ought to. Jet is a stone that will help give you the courage to move forward, which is why it's used for prosperity work.

Kyanite: ranges in colour from denim to sapphire blue. Kyanite can be used for emotional healing or to strengthen your resolve and increase your self-confidence. It can also be used to help you look at past events rationally, without anger or sorrow. Kyanite can be used with the Releasing Past Hurts exercise.

Lapis Lazuli: is a deep blue crystal flecked with white and gold. Lapis Lazuli is thought to stimulate the higher levels of the mind encouraging clarity and objectivity. It's also believed to allow the release of stress, bringing deep inner peace. Clarity is very useful for any kind of prosperity work.

Lodestone (Magnetite): is a naturally magnetic form of iron ore. It's believed to help draw love, wealth, luck or happiness into your life. It can be used with other crystals to increase their power.

Lodestones should be carried in pairs - one to attract positive energy and one to repel negative energy. Whatever your prosperity aspirations you may find a Lodestone beneficial.

Malachite: ranges from light to dark green in colour. It's a stone of change and transformation. It encourages old traumas and negative experiences to come to the surface so you can release them. Use Malachite with the Releasing Past Hurts exercise.

Moonstone: is a translucent creamy white stone that appears to glow. Moonstone is used to help calm you and prevent over-reaction to situations due to its calming properties. When you're calm you are in a better position to identify what you truly want.

Obsidian: is a form of volcanic glass. The colour is usually black, silvery or brown, but may also be blue, green, purple or red. It's good for grounding excess energy. This crystal will help balance you, which is a good starting point for beginning prosperity work.

Onyx: is a form of Chalcedony, a crystal made up of many fine layers of sub-microscopic grains of Quartz. The colours range from white to almost every colour.

Onyx is reputed to bring unexpected good luck and opportunity to its owner. It's also reputed to protect its owner from the ill wishes of their enemies. Once you've placed you cosmic order an onyx may help you manifest your goals.

Peridot: is also known as Olivine or Chrysolite. It's usually bottle, olive or yellow-green in colour. It has the power to cleanse the heart of resentment, anger, jealousy, bitterness, hatred and greed. Therefore, this stone is good at dealing with past hurts and can help if you are not naturally a giver. A balance of inflow and outflow energy is essential for manifesting abundance.

Pyrite: is also known as 'Fool's Gold'. This is an iron ore, with a deceptive golden sheen. It can be used to help increase the flow of energy and break through energy blockages. As energy blockages are known to hinder manifestation, Pyrite is a useful stone to own. It will help balance your inflow and outflow energy.

Rhodochrosite: is also known as Raspberry or Manganese Spar. It's a striking raspberry pink colour and is a stone of love and passion. It's believed to have the power to attract one's soul mate, which is helpful if that is one of your goals. It also stimulates the mind and encourages creativity, which may be helpful when trying to decide what's important to you.

Ruby: has a range of colours from pinkish-red to red. Ruby brings integrity, devotion and happiness. It also enhances generosity and brings prosperity. Therefore, a ruby is an excellent stone for any kind of prosperity work.

Sapphire: is a beautiful gemstone ranging from pale lilac to deepest midnight. It can also be found in yellow, black, white and a rare red-orange coloured variety. Known as a 'peace-maker', Sapphire is reputed to create a harmonious atmosphere in any room, making it a useful stone for prosperity work.

Smokey Quartz: is a transparent Quartz crystal that is dark brown, grey brown or black in colour. It's useful for clarity of purpose, careful planning, patience, commitment and grounding excess energy. As patience is often required in prosperity work a Smokey Quartz is a useful crystal to have.

Tiger's Eye: is most commonly golden-brown in colour, but it may also be red, blue or black. Tiger's Eye has traditionally been used to attract abundance, good luck and wealth. This crystal is a good all-rounder for prosperity work.

Topaz: comes in yellow, brown, blue, colourless or pink. It's said to manifest wealth and health as long as your desires are for the greater good. This is a great stone to have providing you are not requesting anything that will harm someone else.

Using Crystals

There are many ways to use your crystals. Here are some suggestions:

Wear them in your socks/shoes so the beneficial properties can help your physical health

Place them in the bath

Make an elixir by soaking your crystal in a bowl of water for twenty-four hours. Drink the elixir for an energy supercharge. You may prefer to put it in a spray bottle and spray your home, money, workplace or purse/wallet

Wear the crystals as jewellery

Put the stones in your pocket

Place the stones near the front door of your home or workplace

Hang the stones with a green, gold or silver ribbon from the rear-view mirror in your car

Place one or more stones on your desk

Put them in your purse/wallet

Put large stones in the four corners of your home

Place your chosen crystal under your pillow

Wear your chosen crystal in your underwear

Make an indoor or outdoor rock garden

Personally I like to hold crystals in my hand, breathe deeply and then visualise my intention. This method helps to reprogramme your mind with what you want, and programs the crystal as well.

Another powerful technique is to write down what you want to manifest. Then place a Citrine on top of the paper. You might like to try the Citrine Wish List exercise:

Exercise: Citrine Wish List

1. Get a piece of paper and write a list of the things you would like to have in your life

2. When your list is complete, write your full name and then sign the piece of paper. Now record the date and time and date

3. Place a Citrine on top of the paper and watch your dreams come alive

I love working with Citrines. Citrine doesn't hold onto negative energy and is self-cleansing, which makes it an ideal stone for prosperity work.

If this exercise doesn't appeal, you may prefer to try the Abundance Ritual instead.

Exercise: Abundance Ritual Using Crystals

Here is an easy ritual that you can do to shift your own personal prosperity energy. You can do this exercise as often as you like.

1. You will need a Citrine, Pyrite and Jade along with a little pouch to carry them in. Ideally your pouch should be green or gold

2. Write this affirmation on a small piece of paper and put it into the pouch with the stones: "I attract and gratefully receive prosperity, abundance and success in my life."

3. Carry this pouch with you everywhere for a week. Whenever you remember to do it, pull out the crystals, hold them in your hands and restate your affirmation

4. Follow this with a quick 5-10 minute meditation. During your meditation visualise being extremely grateful for the prosperity you already have and what's on its way to you

5. Aim to do this 1-2 times every day for a week

You'll be amazed at the changes in you and the magical prosperity flow that you will set in motion.

Cleansing Crystals

Crystals can attract and absorb positive and negative vibrations. Therefore, it's crucial to cleanse them on a regular basis to remove any negative energy.

It's also important to cleanse your crystals before you use them for the first time. They may have travelled thousands of miles, and will probably have been touched by many hands. In order for your crystals to work for you it's important to have just your energy on them.

There are many methods of cleansing crystals; simply choose the one that suits you best. Never cleanse crystals in detergent or soap. Here are some suggestions for cleansing your crystals:

Hold them under running water. The sea, spring, stream or waterfall is best, but spring water will be fine. Allow your crystals to dry naturally (preferably in the sun, as this reenergises them).

Fill a large bowl with cold or tepid water. Add a handful of sea salt to the water and immerse the crystals for a few hours. Rinse your crystals thoroughly afterwards as the salt can damage fragile stones. Allow the crystals to dry naturally.

Rub a few drops on holy water on your crystals to purify them. Allow the crystals to dry naturally.

If you prefer earth cleansing, bury your crystals in the garden for at least 24 hours. Rinse thoroughly in pure water and allow the crystals to dry naturally.

Surround your crystals with night-lights. Leave the night lights to burn out.

Create a smudge-stick. Lightly bind bundles of plant material – usually sage, lavender, cedar or sweet grass. Light the smudge-stick at one end. As it catches fire, blow it out so that it is just smouldering. Slowly rub each crystal in the smoke, ensuring each facet is treated.

Pink rose petals are ideal for cleansing rose quartz. Lavender is good for cleansing amethyst. Collect some petals and flowers, and place them in a glass container. Bury your crystals in the petals or flowers and leave them there for 24 hours. You could then leave the crystals outside to be bathed in sunlight or moonlight (if it's a full moon).

To cleanse your crystals using rice, fill a glass bowl with organic, uncooked brown rice and bury the crystals in the rice. Leave for twenty-four hours. Note: discard this rice after cleansing. Don't be tempted to eat it.

You may prefer mantra cleansing. Either say your own mantra or simply repeat 'Om' to cleanse your crystals. As you repeat 'Om' visualise the negative energies in your crystal being replaced by pure energies.

Finally, you may prefer angelic cleansing. Place your hands lightly on your crystals and call on Archangel Zadkiel and the Ascended Master Saint Germain. Ask them to transform any negativity into positive light energy. Visualise your crystal surrounded by a violet flame of purification.

After cleansing your crystals you need to dedicate your crystals. This protects the crystals from anyone who may try to abuse their power. It also ensures the crystals will only be used in a positive way for the highest good.

To dedicate and protect your crystals, hold them in your hands and visualise them protected by light. Say "I dedicate this stone to be used for the Universal good".

"The future belongs to those who believe in the beauty of their dreams."
Eleanor Roosevelt

11. Prosperity Herbs and Foods

Contrary to popular belief, using plants, herbs and foods to manifest abundance is not a new-age idea. Plants of all kinds (including trees), herbs and roots have been used for prosperity work for centuries. Plants can be used to draw money to a person or to bring prosperity to their home.

There are several ways to use plants in prosperity work: I have suggested the most common uses in this chapter. You may like to do your own research about the link between prosperity and food.

You can carry herbs. Put a tiny bit of the herb in a plastic bag and put in your pocket. Alternatively, you can put a pinch of the herb into a locket.

You may prefer to sew a pouch for your prosperity herbs. If you want to make your own pouch use green or yellow fabric. These colours are associated with prosperity and money.

You can tuck your pouch under the bed or somewhere in your home. You can wear your pouch on a string around your neck. You may prefer to put it in your purse or wallet. Some people prefer to fill a potpourri jar with the appropriate herbs and leave it in a prominent place. It's a matter of personal choice.

The simplest 'Earth, Water, Air, Fire Ritual' is to boil your herb for a while in water. The herbs represent the element of earth. The water element is the water in the pot. The air element is the steam and the fire element is the stove.

If you want to do this ritual, occasionally stir the herb in the water while thinking of your prosperity goals. Strain the herb and sprinkle it around your home or outside your home.

You can also use herbs as incense. Some plants are hypnotics so only use them as incense if you are certain that the herb is not toxic once set alight.

Here are some of the most popular herbs used to draw prosperity and abundance.

Prosperity Herbs

This list isn't conclusive. However, these are the most common prosperity herbs:

Alfalfa - also known as the "good luck" herb. Tuck a sprig of this in your purse or in a locket. If you combine Alfalfa with other money drawing herbs in a sachet it's believed to reinforce the powers.

Allspice - can be carried, burned as incense or sprinkled in the four corners of your house. It's believed to attract business luck or success. It's still important to tell the Universe what you want.

Basil - soak basil leaves in water for three days. Then sprinkle the water at your workplace. This is thought to attract financial success. Note: make sure some of the basil infused water is sprinkled around the entrance as all prosperity needs to cross your threshold.

Bayberry – can be bought as a candle. This is believed to bring luck to your home and put money in your pocket. Bayberry can also be bought as incense.

Bay Leaves - increase intuition and are good if you're looking for a promotion or a new job. Tuck some Bay Leaves under your mattress or boil them and sprinkle the water around your home. Don't burn Bay Leaves.

Catnip - is used for legal confrontations, contracts and the signing of documents. It lends itself well to matters of money and winning arguments.

Chamomile - drinking the tea is thought to bring luck and prosperity. It also helps induce relaxation. The more relaxed and open to prosperity you are the more you will manifest.

Cinnamon - can be used in cooking. Simply add a pinch in your cooking to manifest quick money. Cinnamon can also be bought as incense or burned on charcoal. You can also sprinkle it in your wallet or cash register to attract business.

Citronella - the leaves are thought to be good for attracting business. Either carry some citronella leaves or place them at the entrance to your workplace.

Cloves - can be burned on charcoal or put in your purse or wallet to draw money to you. An ancient money and protection ritual is to stick the heads of cloves into an orange. This is tied with a ribbon and hung in the kitchen. This is done to ensure your cupboards are never bare.

Dill – can be carried to assist in matters of contract. It's also thought to be a good herb for those wishing to attract love. Remember to tell the Universe what you want.

Honeysuckle - live and dried flowers are used to attract luck business and prosperity.

Juniper berries - are said to attract luck, good fortune and business success.

Lavender - is best known for its properties of contentment, balance, love and good health. Lavender can also be used to keep your home in balance. It's a wonderful all round herb.

Lemon Verbena – put into sachets to attract love.

Marjoram – is used to bring about happiness, money, prosperity and health. It's a good general prosperity herb

Mint - is used to attract good spirits and speed good fortune to the bearer. I always grow a pot of mint by my backdoor

Nutmeg - if often added to prosperity herb mixes. It reinforces the manifestation power of your wishes.

Parsley - is used for purification and protection. The purer your thoughts the more you are likely to manifest.

Patchouli - can be added to prosperity herb mixes to reinforce the manifestation power of your wishes. Patchouli can also be burned as incense.

Rosemary - is used as a smudge or dried and sprinkled on coal to release the smoke to purify an area. Rosemary has great healing properties. Sometimes healing is required before prosperity and abundance can manifest in your life.

Sage - is often bundled tightly into smudge sticks and burned as a scent to increase psychic awareness and provide protection.

St John's Wort – rub the dried leaves on your wrists and temples to calm you and reduce anxiety. Some say you should sleep on a sachet of St. John's Wort and Sage to bring on prophetic dreams.

Thyme – is often dried and used for healing, psychic awareness and purification. Thyme can also be used for attracting love.

Yarrow - hang this in bundles to demonstrate your gratitude. It's often used to give thanks for life and spiritual energy. Gratitude is hugely important in prosperity work, so if nothing else hang a bunch of Yarrow in your home.

There are various ways of using prosperity herbs. However you choose to use your herbs bless them first. This adds strength to their beneficial properties. Ways to use your herbs include:

Hang herb sprigs from the rear-view mirror in your car

Decorate your kitchen with dried herb sprigs

Carry them in your pocket

Sprinkle powdered herbs around the inside and outside of your home and workplace

Use them in potpourri

Write your affirmations on the outside of a plant pot with a permanent marker. Grow your favourite herb in the plant pot

Create infusions for using in the bath or washing the floor

Season salads with them

Use them in cooking

Grow them in your garden for prosperity and abundance in your physical environment

Prosperity Foods

There are lots of foods considered lucky.

In many places, foods shaped like coins are thought to bring prosperity in the New Year. Some believe eating green vegetables, such as cabbage, chard, or kale helps prosperity. Eating folded greens at New Year is thought to represent money and bring good fortune.

In Spain, Portugal, Mexico, Cuba, Ecuador, and Peru, it's traditional to eat 12 grapes at midnight on New Year's Eve. This is thought to represent one grape for each month in the coming year. Some people say the name of the month as they eat each grape. If that grape is sweet, it will be a good month.

Pork is a symbol of prosperity in many cultures. Pigs are considered good luck because they root forward, symbolising progress. The fatty meat is also symbolic of fattening wallets in Italy.

Fish scales (especially silver scales), are thought to be a lucky food for the New Year in some places. In Germany some people will put some fish scales in their purse or wallet to bring luck.

The Chinese take prosperity and abundance very seriously. The following are good luck foods associated with the Chinese New Year:

Tangerines and Oranges: Displaying and eating these fruits is said to bring wealth and luck.

Long Noodles: Keep them as long as possible for a long life.

The Tray of Togetherness: This tray is put out for visiting relatives to snack on, or given as a gift. Eight is a traditionally symbolic lucky number, and so the tray contains eight compartments. Each compartment is filled with preserved kumquats for prosperity, coconut for togetherness, longan fruit to bring many sons, and red melon seeds for happiness.

Nian Gao. (year cake): The steamed sweets are made of glutinous rice flour, brown sugar, and oil. Nian Gao symbolises achieving new heights in the coming year.

Pomelo: This large citrus fruit is popular because it's thought to bring continuous prosperity and status.

Jai: This vegetarian dish is eaten because it's part of the Buddhist culture to cleanse yourself with vegetables. It's packed with sea moss for prosperity and lotus seeds for children/birth of sons. It also contains noodles for longevity and lily buds to send 100 years of harmonious union. Chinese black mushrooms are used to fulfil wishes from east to west

Long Leafy Greens and Long Beans: Leafy greens are served whole to wish a long life for parents.

Whole Fish: It's important that the fish is served with the head and tail intact. This is said to ensure a good start and finish to the year, and to avoid bad luck throughout the year.

Sweets: Serving desserts brings a sweet life in the New Year.

Yuanbao (Jiaozi). This is a dumpling dough, which is wrapped around pork and cabbage. Yuanbao (jiaozi) is said to bring prosperity.

There are other foods associated with prosperity and abundance but there wasn't room to include them all. You will find more information by doing a search engine enquiry.

"Food for the body is not enough. There must be food for the soul." Dorothy Day (Women's Rights Activist)

12. Power Animals

Power animals are often referred to as totems. Native Americans believe power animals have their own energy and qualities. For example a heron teaches us to be self-reliant.

This chapter is only intended to be an introduction to power animals. It's a fascinating subject and there's plenty of information available on the internet.

Power animals are accessed in the same ways as other spiritual beings. You can access them through prayer, meditation and visualisation. You may be out walking when a power animal crosses your path. For example a pheasant ran in front of my car this morning. The pheasant tells us that through the use of colour and confidence we can attract what we want.

Like all prosperity work you need to be open to seeing and recognising the messages from the Universe. Your power animal won't appear with a label around its neck. You need to be open to noticing and interpreting the message intended for you.

In this chapter I have listed the power animals most commonly associated with prosperity work. Here are those power animals, and a brief summary of each one:

Ant:
The ant gives you patience, discipline and endurance to make your dreams a reality. The ant brings prosperity and abundance, but first you have to put the work in. The ant is an excellent power animal for long-term plans. It's also a good totem for teamwork.

Bat:
The bat is a symbol of transformation, which can be scary for some people. The bat is great for letting go of your old way of life and embracing something new. The bat is commonly used for spiritual or financial development. If you're in a financial crisis, call on the bat to help you see the way to better financial prosperity.

Bear:
Regardless of which type of bear you encounter, they all represent strength and power. This is often the power to get through your current

difficulties and to then enjoy prosperity and abundance. The bear also represents hidden skills and abilities, which in turn will lead you to prosperity and abundance.

Beaver:
The beaver is by nature a hard worker. Follow the beaver's example of persistence, creativity and inventiveness. All of these lead to greater prosperity and abundance. The beaver reminds you that you have to act on your dreams to make them a reality. This requires a leap of faith.

Bee:
The bee is considered by many to be a symbol of good luck. Not only is it a great pollinator, but it also produces honey, which is associated with the sweetness of life. The bee reminds you to extract the honey of life and to make your life productive while the sun shines. No matter how great your dream is the bee promises fulfilment if you pursue your dreams.

Boar or Pig:
The boar or pig is a very powerful animal totem. It's a totem of prosperity and spiritual strength. It's also a strong protector totem. The boar of pig is encouraging you to develop self-reliance. If you do so you will emerge the conqueror.

Buffalo:
North American Indians believe the buffalo is a powerful totem to have. They believe that anyone with a buffalo totem must walk a sacred path, honouring every walk of life. The buffalo is widely recognised as a totem of abundance, but it's important to be grateful for everything you already have.

Bull or Cow:
Both of these power animals are associated with the zodiac sign of Taurus. It's believed the bull can be helpful in manifesting money and material goods. The cow represents patience, calm and fertility. It tells you to be patient and your dreams will be realised.

Butterfly:
The butterfly represents change, transition and growth. Obviously the form this takes is different for each of us. Butterflies teach that change is positive and should be embraced. Often change leads to greater

prosperity and abundance (not necessarily financial). Butterfly wings tell you that you have the power to fly.

Cat:
Since time began, the cat has always been recognised as a magical and mystical animal. A cat totem encourages agility in both body and mind, which is often needed in prosperity work. If you trust the cat it will help you to be strong and confidant.

Cricket:
In China, the cricket is a symbol of good luck and abundance. In England, it's considered good luck to find a cricket on the hearth. Although the cricket appears to be a small power animal, it has the ability to make giant leaps. Use this message to have the faith to take great leaps into the unknown. You will be rewarded with greater prosperity and abundance.

Cuckoo:
The cuckoo tells us that it's time for new beginnings. The cuckoo is great for encouraging you to trust your intuition more. Many view the cuckoo as a benevolent power animal, which is willing to assist you with your personal transformation.

Deer:
The deer is a symbol of prosperity and abundance to many of the world's people. The deer tells you to be gentle with yourself and others during the unending process of prosperity work. The deer also encourages you to accept yourself as you are. Once you can do this you will find prosperity work much easier, as you remove resistance from your life.

Donkey:
The donkey personifies determination and service to others. The donkey expects you to work for what you get, but it will help you to stay focused and get the job done. Far from being stubborn, donkey's trust, respect and listen to their own intuition. Follow the donkey's example and you won't go far wrong.

Dragon:
There are four types of dragon. These are fire, air, water and earth. Dragons are deemed to be power animals with supreme influence. Dragons have long been associated with all forms of prosperity work.

Dragonfly:
The dragonfly inhabits two realms - air and water. The dragonfly is good for any form of transformation in your life. It's helpful in getting through poverty patterns and reaching a more joyous state.

Eagle:
The eagle is able to soar to great heights. The message it sends is you too can soar to great heights if you have the ability to visualise it. The eagle tells you that you are only limited by your own self-limiting beliefs. You may have noticed that the eagle appears on American dollars. Therefore, it's a useful symbol if you want to invoke for money.

Frog:
The frog is another totem of transformation or metamorphosis. Notice how the frog is able to jump from one thing to another. The frog's message is you can effortlessly jump to the next level of prosperity and abundance. Because of its colour (green), the frog is associated with all forms of prosperity and abundance.

Goat:
The goat often appears in meditations when you're not sure if you're on the right path. The goat tells you to keep moving forward and you will achieve your goals.

The goat is associated with the zodiac sign of Capricorn. It tells you that you have the ability to scale mountains and great obstacles. Stick with it and you will enjoy greater prosperity and abundance.

Grasshopper:
Like the cricket, in China, the grasshopper is a symbol of good luck and abundance. It has the ability to make giant leaps, and tells you to do the same thing. As grasshoppers are generally green or brown they are an excellent totem for manifesting more money or material goods.

Hawk:
All hawks are viewed as great prosperity and abundance totems. Due to their keen eyesight they can see both poverty patterns and new opportunities. Call upon the hawk if you need rapid change to deal with a crisis. The hawk is a very serious and intense energy. Therefore, only ever call on the hawk if you really mean business.

Hummingbird:
The hummingbird inspires gratitude and positive thinking. It encourages you to taste the sweetness of life. The hummingbird also appears on the back of the British £10 with Charles Darwin; making it a powerful money totem.

Kingfisher:
The Kingfisher or the Australian Kookaburra is a symbol of peace and prosperity. The Kingfisher is the promise of abundance. Its blue plumage is associated with Jupiter, the planet of abundance.

Lion:
The male lion is a magnificent animal that has long been associated with power and success. The lion encourages you to use stealth and take the easy way to achieve your goals. The lion will give you confidence to achieve the greatest level of prosperity and abundance.

Phoenix:
We've all heard about the phoenix rising from the ashes to fly once again. The phoenix can be a powerful ally for any major change in your life. It gives you hope in the midst of despair. Some believe the phoenix can be helpful in revitalising your finances.

Rabbit:
Rabbits are often associated with prosperity and abundance due to their ability to procreate in such vast numbers. It may be telling you that your fortunes will move forwards in leaps and bounds. Rabbits sometimes represent positive changes in springtime. Rabbits encourage you to follow their example as this can multiply your own luck many times over.

Snake:
The snake is often associated with transformation and healing. The snake is able to shed its skin and can help you to transform your life current situation into something more positive. If you need help to shed poverty patterns and grow new prosperity habits, call on the snake's energy.

Spider:
The spider has long been associated with creative power and manifestation due to its ability to weave webs. The spider is considered helpful when you need to make new connections. The spider is

considered to be a powerful totem animal for any kind of creative venture or writing.

Turkey:
In America the turkey is a symbol of harvest and the rewards of work well done. The turkey tells you that through giving to others you will reach your own goals.

You may encounter, or feel drawn to, other power animals. If so, listen to your intuition and research the message it's conveying to you. If you would like to find out more about power animals type '[animal name/type] totem animal' into your search engine.

I hope this chapter has opened your mind to the possibility of power animals.

"An animal's eyes have the power to speak a great language." Martin Buber (Jewish Philosopher)

Part Three

"Heaven on earth is a choice you must make; not a place we must find"
Dr Wayne Dwyer

13. Manifesting Your Own Abundance

You can have what you want; unless your aspirations are totally unrealistic of course. It's worth remembering that some people may be able to manifest the top Lottery prize, but not everyone can have it. Of course not everyone wants to win the Lottery.

One of the most important things you can do for yourself is to work out just what it's that you truly want. What is your vision of a prosperous and abundant life? Having goals is essential in prosperity work.

Having a goal gives the Universe something concrete to focus on. You can change your goals as often as you like. However, having a clear goal makes it much easier to manifest what you want. If you don't tell the Universe what you want how will you know if you have what you desire?

Be very clear and specific about what you want to attract. Do you just want to manifest more disposable income or do you want to attract more clients, or get more business from your existing clients?

The clearer you are about your goals the easier it will be for the Universe to deliver what you truly want.

If you cannot define your goals clearly (in writing) you cannot expect to get what you want. The Universe will always try to deliver what you want, but it needs to understand what this is. Manifesting abundance is about team work.

Never ask the Universe to manifest things that you don't genuinely want. Also, never ask the Universe for anything that will harm someone else in the process of delivering what you want. Both create bad karma.

The most common example of this is asking for someone who is already in a relationship with someone else. Wait until the person is available before asking the Universe to bring you together. Note: If the other party doesn't feel the same way you're unlikely to come together.

The other thing you need to be aware of is - you can only make requests for yourself. You cannot request an end to world poverty, exam success for your children, or anything else for others. By submitting requests on behalf of others you're interfering with their energy and life purpose. You don't have the right to do this; no matter how honourable your intentions are.

Although your job is to tell the Universe what you want, it's not your job to worry about how this will be delivered. The steps to manifesting prosperity and abundance are:

1. Decide what you truly want

2. Send the intention to the Universe. The stronger the vibration the sooner you will manifest your heart's desires

3. Take the steps necessary to assist the Universe. We all have a part to play in manifesting our prosperity and abundance

4. Trust the Universe to deliver what you want or something as close as possible

5. Look for signs of your prosperity manifesting and demonstrate your gratitude

If you have already dealt with your self-limiting beliefs then you're in the right place to start manifesting true prosperity and abundance. However, if your inner voice starts to argue with the goals you're setting yourself, acknowledge the resistance and deal with it.

Do a quick reality check to ensure your self-limiting beliefs are a thing of the past. If you find yourself saying "I can't" you're not ready for abundance yet. "I can't" really means "I choose not to" or "I'm afraid". You may have a fear of failure or success. Both need to be addressed before you can move forward.

If your subconscious is still resistant talk to your higher self like a mother gently talking to a child. Ensure your tone is kind and not challenging, as change is scary to your subconscious.

Imagine you're holding the child's hand, look up to the Universe and say "I [your name] need to ask you subconscious why we need to feel [state what your concern or resistance is]".

Listen to the voice in your head and then say "I understand your concerns, but it's safe for us to accept this change. This change is going to bring good health, happiness, wealth etc".

Don't beat yourself up about any goals not yet achieved, or recurring themes in your life. Life is a journey and a learning experience, not a punishment. Remember you're here for a good time not a long time. Every experience, good or bad, is a lesson for you.

Manifesting prosperity and abundance is a choice you can make at any time in your life. You may have to accept that now is not the right time for you. If so, come back to it another time.

If now is the right time, there are lots of different ways to request and manifest the things you truly want. The first example I have detailed is the Wish List Exercise.

Exercise: Wish List

Imagine the world is your oyster. Be creative and draw up your own wish list of goals. Work on this exercise every day for at least a week.

1. Get a piece of paper and create a bucket list. These are things you would like to have or achieve before you die

2. From this list create a new list of everything you would like to manifest now or as soon as possible

3. We will deal with these first. Next to each item identify what is stopping you having what you desire. Perhaps your subconscious is telling you that you can't have a new car. Maybe you're hearing "I can't have a new car as I don't earn enough money"

4. Look at each excuse you have written about why you can't have what you want. Explain the rationale behind your thinking. For example "I'm afraid to hope that I will earn enough to buy a new car in case I fail"

5. Now you understand the rationale for your thinking you're on the way to success. Now state "I release my negative and self-limiting beliefs. They no longer serve a purpose for me". Of course you need to mean it, not simply pay lip service to this

6. At the end of the week across the top of the page write CLEARED AND RELEASED. You can now tear up these sheets, or light a candle and burn them. These self-limiting thoughts no longer have power over you

It doesn't matter if you fail to manifest all the things on your wish list. It hasn't happened for one of the following reasons:

Reason 1 - it wasn't really that important to you

Reason 2 - you're not ready for what you have asked for, or it's not the right time

Reason 3 - during the process your needs and wants changed

Reason 4 - you did not state your desired outcome clearly enough for the Universe to deliver what you wanted

This exercise is excellent for people new to prosperity work. It tests your self-limiting beliefs and gets you thinking about what you really want.

Doing this exercise doesn't mean that you will get a new car, or anything else you want, instantly. The Universe will deliver your cosmic order when the time is right and if the vibration is strong enough.

In my case, I had to wait many years before I could afford to buy a new car. Since then the Universe has made it possible for me to have several new cars (three of them were Volkswagen Beetles). My patience was more than well rewarded by the Universe.

This exercise has shown you what is holding you back. Keep repeating this exercise until you overcome any self-limiting beliefs that are still holding you back.

When you're ready and free of self-limiting beliefs start manifesting. More importantly, enjoy everything you receive and be grateful for it.

Another way to manifest true prosperity and abundance is to visualise your prosperity story. Everyone's idea of prosperity and abundance is different so it's important that your vision reflects what you want.

Don't make your vision what others suggest you want. It's a natural human failing to tell others what they should have, but you must ignore others and do what's right for you.

Exercise: My Personal Prosperity Story

1. Sit or lie somewhere comfortable. Choose somewhere you won't be disturbed

2. Breathe in deeply through your nose and slowly exhale through your mouth

3. Repeat this deep breathing exercise for a couple of minutes until you feel yourself relaxing. You may start to feel lightheaded or less grounded

4. With your next breath, imaging yourself sitting in a huge bubble of white or golden light. This bubble is protecting you from harm

5. Tell yourself a story or visualise what it would be like for you to experience perfect abundance. Don't worry about whether any of this is possible or how you're going to manifest it. This is just a story at this stage

6. Mentally phrase your story as if all of this is currently taking place in your life. Instead of saying "I would love to have a holiday home in Spain" say "I am now spending 3, 6, or 9 months each year in my lovely holiday home in Spain"

7. If any doubts creep into your mind, simply tell yourself "All things are possible through the divine spirit in me". Then return to your story

8. When you have completed your story, say a little prayer of thanks to the Universe for making this dream life possible

9. End with the following affirmation "All things are possible through the divine spirit within me"

You may struggle to get started with your story. If so, here are some things to think about for your story:

Who else features in your story (maybe your husband, wife, partner, children, friends etc)?

Are you rich beyond your wildest dreams or just comfortably off? Perhaps money doesn't matter to you at all

What kind of work are you doing, if any?

What interests are you pursuing (career or hobbies)?

How are you spending your time?

How much free time do you have?

Do you have any health problems?

What material things do you have in your dream life (e.g. a holiday home abroad)?

Where are you in your spiritual life?

Write your story down, record it onto a CD or YouTube, or simply visualise it in your mind. Choose whichever option gives you the clearest picture of your ideal life.

When creating your personal prosperity story declare what you want. Never include the things you don't want. Also, never say "I really want...." or "I don't want"; instead say "I have...." or "thank you for...." Always focus on the positive things you want, as if you already have them.

Return to your story regularly and fine tune it. When you're ready release your thoughts to the Universe. If possible, try not to declare a timescale as the Universe prefers to work at its own pace not yours.

If neither of the previous exercises appeal to you try the massive goal exercise instead.

Setting a goal doesn't commit you to this permanently. You're free to change your goals at any time. Goal setting techniques are used by top-level athletes, successful business-people and achievers in all fields. It helps them focus on what they truly want to achieve. If it works for them it can work for you too.

Some believe the bigger the goal the greater the success you will achieve. Even if you don't manifest exactly what you asked for you will achieve more than if you set a small goal.

Exercise: Create a Massive Goal

Set an absolutely massive goal for yourself. Your goal needs to be so big that if achieved it will blow your mind. For example; from your new business idea to the level of business success enjoyed by Sir Richard Branson.

This is real blue sky thinking. If you're ready for the challenge try this exercise:

1. Sit comfortably and allow your shoulders to drop so your body knows it's OK to relax

2. Close your eyes. You're always in control so you can return to your awakened state at any time by simply opening your eyes

3. Take a deep breath and then exhale very slowly. As you do this focus on your breathing

4. Repeat this deep breathing until you feel relaxed

5. Continue the deep breathing, but as you do so think about your massive goal. Do you want to own one of the top 100 companies, become an airline pilot, or invent something that will bring you fame and fortune? The list is endless

6. Declare your massive goal to the Universe. Be very clear about what you want. The more detailed your vision the more you will achieve

7. Make sure your aspirations are written in the present tense e.g. "I have..., I receive..., I am..." Include words that convey positive, energetic feelings e.g. "It's fantastic that..., I am delighted to......., I am so happy that...." Remember, the Universe responds to what it thinks you already have and assumes you want more of the same

8. Don't set a timeline; just trust the process to work for you at the right time. The stronger the vibration the quicker your goal will manifest

9. Visualise what it looks like, as if you have already achieved it. Experience it in detail

10. Truly believe that you're worthy of what you have declared as your massive goal

11. Let the Universe decide how your goal will be fulfilled. Unlike conventional goal setting, it's not your job to decide how your prosperity and abundance should manifest

12. Release your request to the Universe and know that it will manifest at the right time

13. Revisit your massive goal regularly. You're doing this to strengthen the vibration. It's also an opportunity to confirm you still want this goal. If not, change your goal to what you do want

14. Feel gratitude for what you already have and become more grateful as you manifest your dream life. Gratitude encourages the Universe to give you even more

If you think goals this big don't happen then you don't know John Assaraf's story.

John tells the story about an incident that occurred in May 2000. He was working in his home office in his beautiful new home in Southern California. His five-year old son came in and asked him what was in the dusty boxes in the corner of his home office.

John told him that they contained his Vision Boards (Prosperity Wheels). His son didn't understand what they were, so John opened one of the boxes to show him. When John pulled out the second collage from the box, he began to cry.

On this Prosperity Wheel was a picture of a 7,000 square foot house on top of six acres of spectacular land. John had seen this picture in the Dream Homes magazine in 1995. He had cut the picture out and stuck it on his collage.

In 1995 this was a massive goal.

"We can have whatever it is we choose, I don't care how big it is." John Assaraf

Another type of manifesting prosperity and abundance is the vision of my life. This type of manifesting requires setting a variety of goals from now until the end of your life.

Exercise: The Prosperity and Abundance Vision of My Life

For this exercise you will need short-term goals (the next 3 months), medium term goals (the next 1-2 years) and long-term goals (things you want to manifest before you die).

1. Get three sheets of paper. On the first sheet write the heading 'Short-term Goals'. On the second sheet write the heading 'Medium-term Goals', and on the third sheet write 'Long-term Goals

2. On your short-term goals sheet create a list of the things you want to manifest in the next three months. This could be a mini break with loved ones or friends, passing an exam, more me-time or anything else you want

3. On your second sheet create a list of the things you want to manifest in the next one to two years. These will probably be bigger goals like buying a new car or moving house. The potential list is endless

4. On the final sheet create a list of all the things you would like to manifest or achieve before you die. Think of this as your bucket list. Do you want go on a luxury cruise, have children etc?

5. You can add new goals, amend or remove existing ones at any time. This is a living document and should be updated to reflect your changing needs/wants

6. Review your short-term goals daily to strengthen the vibration. This will enable you to see what you're manifesting. It will also show you how your requirements are changing over time

7. Review your medium and long-term goals periodically

8. At each review amend, add or delete items. It's fine to leave your list unchanged too (but this rarely happens)

9. At some point in the future review your goals. You may do this in several months or years. You may choose to do it more than once - it's just a visualisation exercise. Imagine you're now on your deathbed. Did you achieve all your goals? Did the things that matter to you change over time?

Creating a visual picture of your own prosperity and abundance is a powerful way to bring it to you. The more clearly you can imagine this the greater the chances of success.

Another way to manifest the prosperity and abundance you want it to create your own personal Prosperity Wheel. These are also known as vision boards, treasure maps, visual explorers or creativity collages.

A prosperity wheel is a collage of pictures and affirmations that represent your personal vision of true prosperity and abundance. The idea is when you surround yourself with images of what you want your life changes to match those desires.

Prosperity wheels are fun to do. This visual image of your desires is a constant reminder to you and the Universe. It encourages you to focus on prosperity, abundance and happiness instead of misery lack and scarcity.

I have published a book devoted entirely to prosperity wheels. If you're interested, the book is called Create Your Own Prosperity Wheel (A step-by-step guide to using the Law of Attraction to manifest the things you want). For now, here are the instructions to create a prosperity wheel.

Exercise: Create a Prosperity Wheel (Vision Board)

Buy a large piece of coloured card. The only other materials you require for creating a prosperity wheel are a good selection of magazines, scissors, glue, a pen and a photograph of yourself.

For any form of prosperity work it's important to get yourself into the right frame of mind before you start. Therefore, I suggest you do a short meditation to clear your mind.

As you meditate set the intent for the session. Ask yourself what it is that you truly want in your life e.g. a holiday, love, a new home, a car, a job, holiday home, a baby etc. The answer may come to you as single words, statements or images

Now you're ready to start. Play your favourite music in the background and just enjoy the process. This really is a fun way to manifest the prosperity and abundance you truly want and deserve.

1. Look through each magazine. Pull out any pictures, words or headlines that appeal to you or represent the things you want in your life. Choose big, bright and colourful pictures. Small, drab pictures will achieve small results (the Universe likes colour)

2. Make a big pile of images, phrases and words. Don't worry if some are duplicates, you can discard the ones you don't want later

3. When you've finished go through your pile of pictures and eliminate any images that no longer feel right. This step is where your intuition comes in. As you go through the pictures, you'll get a sense what you want and don't want

4. At the top of your card write "I am worthy of the best the Universe can offer". Make this statement large enough to be read easily

5. In the middle of your collage put a photograph of yourself. Ideally you should be looking radiant and happy, and staring at the camera. Happiness is the message you want to send to the Universe

6. Lay your pictures and headlines on the board. As you do this you will get a sense of how the board should be laid out. Only include images that represent the things you want in your life

7. All of your images should form a circle around the photograph of you. Stick the images onto the card when you're happy with your choices

8. Next, you need to make a link between each image and you. To do this, draw a strong line from you to the image. It will eventually look like the spokes of a wheel

9. Now you need to write a relevant affirmation for each image. Write your affirmation on the line you have just drawn. Be sure to write your 'affirmations' in the present tense

10. At the bottom of your collage write "these things or something better now manifest for me in easy and pleasant ways for the highest good of all concerned". It's important to add this note to your prosperity wheel. This tells the Universe you don't want to get things at the expense of harming someone else. For example, you don't want to break up someone's marriage etc

You now need to decide where you're going to display your prosperity wheel. Some say it should be hidden away so others cannot mock it or interfere with it. Others say it should be visible to strengthen your desire and intention. Personally, I always hang mine on the study wall.

There are areas of houses which don't have the correct flow of 'chi' to promote prosperity everywhere. If you don't know the Feng Shui of where you live, your best bet is to put the wheel next to a door into a room, or on the door. This is known as 'the gateway of chi' and is a neutral area which will not interfere with the energies of your prosperity wheel.

You can create a new prosperity wheel anytime your goals change. You can keep adding to it (if there's sufficient space), or you can even just change the pictures. This is your vision, and so it needs to work for you.

John Assaraf brought the age-old concept of a Vision Board (Prosperity Wheel) into the public eye by telling his story in 'The Secret'. He has a series of these collages that he has been creating over many years. Periodically he looks at them to remind himself of all the things he has manifested in his life.

Your current level of prosperity and abundance is directly related to your previous thoughts and words. Throughout your life the Universe has been listening to your instructions. Everything you currently have, or don't have, is a direct response to earlier requests.

If you don't like what you currently have, or you're not getting what you want from life, change it. Define what you want, request it and believe it's going to be yours.

The words you choose have a direct impact on the level of prosperity and abundance you create for yourself. If you keep saying "I'm broke, I wish I had some money" you will continue to create scarcity

If however, you say "I'm prosperous and successful" you will manifest abundance. This statement may not be true initially. If you believe it and visualise what you want, and you can make it happen.

Talk positively to yourself every day. Tell yourself how prosperous you are and how easily money flows to you.

If your aspirations are career related tell yourself how effortlessly you achieve success in the workplace. If your focus is on health and wellbeing tell yourself that you're fit and healthy. No matter what you want, tell yourself that you've already got it.

This regular self-talk is particularly important if you haven't manifested your goals yet. This will help to keep you focused and motivated.

It takes approximately 30 days to form a habit. This is just the starting point though. You will need to affirm your prosperity and abundance for the rest of your life to maintain true abundance. If your thinking (vibration) slips back to negative the Universe will think you're no longer interested in prosperity and abundance.

Sometimes abundance manifests immediately, but not always. The Universe will manifest things when the time is right; not necessarily when you want it. The stronger your vibration the sooner it will happen.

How will you know you've started manifesting prosperity and abundance? There are various ways you could become aware. An idea may come into your head, you may have a 'gut' feeling about something, or something may happen unexpectedly. When this happens, watch and see what unfolds.

Sometimes it's not this obvious so be aware of what is going on around you. Answers may come to you in the form of throw away comments from friends or a tune on the radio. The more open and receptive you are to Universal energy, the sooner you will become aware of your new prosperity and abundance.

Gratitude

Gratitude really is the stuff true prosperity and abundance is made of. In fact, gratitude is probably the most important part of prosperity work. When you're filled with gratitude you remove the fear and become an open channel for prosperity energy.

Never underestimate the power of a grateful heart when it comes to manifesting prosperity and abundance. No matter how little you currently have always remember to be grateful. Even feel grateful for the lessons you're learning from your current situation.

Unfortunately, we often take our health, family, friends and material goods for granted. We focus on what we want to manifest, but forget to be grateful for what we already have. Start the gratitude process by acknowledging what you already have.

You may not have a lot of money right now, but I'm sure you have things to be grateful for. Do you have good health, a wonderful spouse, children or people who care about you? All of these should be acknowledged before you start wishing for other things.

Exercise: Daily Gratitude

It's important to get into the habit of daily gratitude. Here's an exercise to start you off.

1. Before going to sleep, or every morning before you get out of bed, think of at least ten things that you're grateful for

2. It can be the same ten or different gratitude's each day. The important thing is to do the exercise

This exercise is great for changing a negative mindset to a positive one.

Developing an attitude of gratitude is a powerful tool. It will have a profound effect on you, which you may not be aware of initially.

The more grateful you feel for everything you already have the happier you feel. This happiness brings a sense of peace and contentment. This new found peace and contentment makes you relax (without you consciously doing it). The more relaxed you are the more prosperity and abundance you will manifest.

You may like to create a gratitude list that you can review and add to each day. Alternatively, spend a few minutes at the end of each day saying or thinking about the things you're grateful for. For example, your health, your ability to read and write, a safe home with clean running water etc.

Whenever you see a sign that your abundance is increasing, even a very small sign, acknowledge it. Be grateful for all your material possessions, your health, your body, your wealth, your life, the people in your life, the air you breathe. In fact be grateful for everything you have.

Exercise: Say 'Thank You' and Mean It

Here is another gratitude exercise that you might like to adopt.

1. Say 'thank you' consciously to everyone you can. Say thank you if someone holds the door open for you, or allows you to filter into the traffic stream

2. Look them in the eye and mean it when you say thank you

3. Watch their response. Many will be pleasantly surprised. Your gratitude makes them grateful too. They are grateful for your acknowledgement

Sticking with gratitude; here is another gratitude exercise you might like to try. It costs nothing to say 'thank you' to someone, but the effect can be significant. We all like to be appreciated. Thank you is a way of making someone feel appreciated for whatever small gesture they made.

Exercise: Thank You

Thank you is a very powerful gratitude message.

1. Write 100 thank yous for a week. It can be the same thank you or different ones

2. Your thank yous might be things you enjoy looking at or enjoy listening to. It could also be things you enjoy touching or feeling, things you like to eat, scents that you like. The list is endless, just be creative.

I always say thank you when the buzzards fly above my home as these are important power animals

3. The more you demonstrate gratitude, the more abundance will come to you

If you don't want to create your own words of gratitude you might like to recite Brian Hinkle's Gratitude Prayer instead:

Exercise: The Gratitude Prayer

Simply read and feel Brian Hinkle's gratitude prayer every day. Don't just say the words. It's important to feel grateful too.

I thank you God/Goddess
I thank you Jesus
I thank the Higher Power
I thank the Ascended Masters
I thank you Saint Francis
I thank you Saint Germaine
I thank all those who guide me through my lives
And I send my loving gratitude
To each and every living creature
Amen

The more grateful you are the more prosperity and abundance you will manifest as like attracts like. Aside from manifesting more you will have a greater sense of wellbeing. This is priceless.

"When our minds are resonating with gratitude the gate is fully opened to the flow of prosperity." Dr Darryl Pokea

14. Conclusion

Prosperity and abundance is a journey, not a destination. We all start at a different place and arrive at a different destination. There is no right or wrong point.

Prosperity and abundance is a wholly personal experience. You can't judge your progress by comparing yourself to others. Prosperity isn't about where you are; it's about how far you've come.

Manifesting prosperity and abundance is no different to learning to play an instrument, ride a bicycle, or learning any other skill. The more effort you put in the more you will manifest.

Developing prosperity consciousness takes time. It also takes a reasonable amount of effort to maintain. It's not something you do once and then forget about it. The potential to manifest prosperity and abundance is limitless.

Those people who are masters of attracting prosperity and abundance share a common trait. They visualise, visualise, visualise and believe absolutely.

The reward for their effort is unlimited prosperity and abundance. Most share their good fortune through their philanthropic work. Aside from financial prosperity and material goods, prosperity brings a wonderful sense of wellbeing. It's quite unlike any other experience.

The prosperity and abundance you're enjoying now is just a fraction of what you could manifest. If you make prosperity and abundance a part of your daily life the benefits will radiate into every aspect of your life.

I would just like to recap on the basic principles of prosperity and abundance:

1. You deserve the best the Universe can offer. The Universe has never asked you to struggle. If you are struggling it's your choice

2. There is no need for anyone to struggle, financially or otherwise. This is a decision made by your conscious or unconscious state. Why inflict unnecessary pain on yourself?

3. True prosperity is always a win/win outcome. If you're wealthy and purchase goods you help someone else prosper. We don't all want the same level of prosperity

4. Poverty won't make you a better person. It will only make you an unhappy person. Who enjoys being unhappy?

5. Prosperity is relevant. What's prosperity to one person may be poverty to someone else. Therefore, focus on what prosperity means to you. Don't worry about other people

6. Being prosperous involves giving, receiving, sharing, accepting compliments and spotting opportunities. The Universe can't do it all; you have to give the Universe a helping hand

7. Worrying about lack of money or anything else doesn't create prosperity and abundance. This just creates more scarcity as this is the vibration you're creating

8. All prosperity is limitless and comes from the same source. There's more than enough to go round. The problem is most people don't know how to ask for it

9. Be very clear about what you want, and what part you're willing to play to make it happen. It's no good saying you want your dream job if you don't apply for it

10. Believe 100% that your dreams will come true. Doubt creates negative energy. Negativity will impact the outcome

11. Review your goals regularly. This will help you to recognise when your prosperity is increasing and ensure your goals are still relevant

12. Gratitude is the most important part of prosperity work. Be grateful for everything you manifest. Gratitude ensures a continuous flow of prosperity and abundance

The subject of prosperity and abundance is huge. There are thousands of books and unlimited information on the internet. I hope I've introduced you to the concept of prosperity and abundance, or some elements of you weren't aware of.

I also hope 'Creating Prosperity and Abundance' has given you food for thought. You may not agree with everything I've written in this book.

Hopefully Creating Prosperity and Abundance' will encourage you to open your mind to the possibilities waiting for you.

Chinese proverb - "If you want 1 year of prosperity, grow grain. If you want 10 years of prosperity, grow trees. If you want 100 years of prosperity, grow people."

If you have your own prosperity story that you would like to share with me, please get in touch. My email address is - shepherdcreativelearning@gmail.com

Here's wishing you prosperity and abundance beyond your wildest dreams!

www.ingramcontent.com/pod-product-compliance
Lightning Source LLC
Chambersburg PA
CBHW060306050426
42448CB00009B/1756